210

Victor A. Lillich
Jan 22, 1959
Seminary / Hoyer
Course No. 570

D1134801

WORSHIP AND THE MODERN CHILD

BY THE SAME AUTHOR

God and His World (s.p.c.k. and n.s.)
The Life of our Lord (s.p.c.k. and n.s.)
Children's Hour Prayers (s.c.m.)
Listen on Wednesday (s.c.m.)
Switch on for the News (s.c.m.)
Where do I Begin? (b.c.c.)
What Next? (s.p.c.k.)
Leading School Worship (s.p.c.k.)

WORSHIP
AND THE
MODERN CHILD

A Book for
Parents, Clergy, and Teachers

By the Reverend
JOHN G. WILLIAMS

With a Foreword by the Bishop of Warrington

LONDON
NATIONAL SOCIETY
S · P · C · K
1957

First published 1957
Reprinted 1958
S.P.C.K.
Holy Trinity Church
Marylebone Road
*London N.W.*1

Made and printed in Great Britain by
William Clowes and Sons, Limited
London and Beccles

© *John G. Williams*, 1957

FOR OUR OWN CHILDREN

CHRISTOPHER

BERNARD and MARTIN

AND IN

MEMORY OF THEIR SISTER

MARGARET

WHO DIED ON 28 FEBRUARY 1954

AGED 8

Thou, O God, hast made us for thyself, and our
hearts are restless till they rest in thee.

PRAYER OF ST AUGUSTINE OF HIPPO

The chief end of man is to glorify God and enjoy
him for ever.

THE SHORTER CATECHISM

CONCORDIA UNIVERSITY LIBRARY
PORTLAND, OR 97211

Contents

Foreword

ONE of the most baffling problems that continue to confront the Church is the alarming fact that so many of the children baptized at our fonts and enrolled in our Sunday Schools fail to take their place as they grow up in the worship and fellowship of the Church. We are familiar with the statistics that were produced some years ago (p. 138). There are grounds to fear that the situation has further deteriorated. The last few years have brought increasing temptations in the form of Television, Sunday cinemas, Sunday joy-rides, to distract children from the worship of the Church and regular instruction in Sunday School. In addition, the sad neglect of family worship and family prayers accounts for a large number of children who have drifted outside the direct influence of the Church. It is true that children in our Day Schools share in a daily act of worship, but this is no substitute for that neglect of Sunday worship which is a distressing sign of our modern age.

John Williams is well qualified to write upon the subject of "Worship and the Modern Child". His ten years of experience with the B.B.C., his subsequent work with the National Society and the Church of England Schools Council, and the fact that he writes as a parish priest have given him a wealth of knowledge and practical experience which is revealed in these pages.

There is no doubt that if the religious education given to children and young people in Day School, Sunday School, and Bible Class is to be effective and lasting, it is primarily necessary that they should be led through it into the fellowship of the Church. A survey undertaken by the University of Leeds revealed that religious education given in Day

Schools is lost by those who receive it by the age of 17 years, unless they have become members of a Church and have a Christian home.

There are certain conditions which should be continually borne in mind, and which are emphasized in this book.

1. The instruction of our children should be broadly based, as the Book of Common Prayer insists, on the Creed, the Lord's Prayer, the Ten Commandments, and the Church Catechism. To neglect this direction is to imperil the fulfilment of our responsibility to children committed to our care.

2. Children and young people must be continually helped and inspired to realize their sense of "belonging" to the Church, which is the heritage given to them at the font.

3. Children should be brought by their parents to the regular service of the Church, including the Holy Communion. The development of "Parish Communions" at which children are present should be encouraged.

4. Children should be genuinely welcomed to the regular services of the Church, even though at times their presence may be a little distracting. Did not our Blessed Lord say, "Suffer the children to come unto me"? I have sometimes asked children whether they enjoy coming to church. Most often they answer, "Yes". When they answer, "No", I suspect that there is something wrong with the church.

5. The P.C.C. of any parish should accept a greater responsibility than many of them do, for the staffing, accommodation, and finance of our Sunday Schools. The shortage of teachers, equipment, and money in the majority of our Sunday Schools is evidence of a lack of care on the part of the Church for the welfare of the children.

This book is addressed to parents, clergy, and teachers. It is to be hoped that it will be widely read and studied. The example of parents in regular attendance at church, and their devotion, in time and understanding, to teaching their children to pray are decisive influences in the life of the child. The imaginative and informed understanding of the child-mind by clergy and teachers who have a clear aim in their teaching can make religious instruction really stimulating and attractive, instead of making it into "dry bones" which were fed to some of us in our youth.

In this book we are given a clear and valuable exposition both of the Church's responsibility towards children committed to her care, and of the child-mind, which will enable parents, clergy, and teachers to fulfil more adequately their task of leading the children into the active fellowship of the Church so that they may "continue Christ's faithful soldiers and servants unto their life's end".

CHARLES WARRINGTON

Introduction

I HAVE been long haunted by a sentence from one of Simone Weil's books: *The danger is not lest the soul should doubt whether there is any bread, but lest, by a lie, it should persuade itself that it is not hungry.* Those pregnant words seem to me to express perfectly the spiritual crisis of the twentieth century. In all previous centuries men have been anxiously concerned to find a satisfactory purpose in their existence. They have in fact been looking for God and for the satisfaction that only God can give. Many of them found the Bread they sought in the Christian Religion, at the hands of him who said, "I am the Bread of Life"; and even those who did not find it there were still conscious of their hunger. However much they were tempted to doubt the existence of the Bread, they still went on feverishly searching for it.

The danger today is that men may abandon the search for Bread because they do not in fact suffer the pangs of hunger. There are drugs, like the benzedrine and dexedrine groups, which can temporarily destroy the appetite and at the same time create an illusory sense of clarity and wellbeing; but the basic needs of the body remain unchanged, and a man who does not eat will die. In much the same way our western scientific civilization, together with all the immense advantages it has brought, has provided us with a host of sensual and intellectual narcotics which can alleviate the pangs of spiritual hunger and produce an illusory sense of wellbeing. At the lowest level we see these drugs at work in the pursuit of purely material and sensational satisfactions—the rising standard of luxury and physical comfort; the host of labour-saving devices; the cinema, the radio, television, the "Pools", and the popular press. The recrudescence of crude, primitive impulses in such degraded dance-forms as Jive, Bebop, and "Rock and Roll" is a disquieting symptom of this narcotic addiction. It is possible for us, if we choose, to fill every leisure moment with some kind of pleasurable and largely sensual gratification, and the deep hunger of the soul is stifled. But the hunger still remains, to break out into an acute agony of craving at times of failure, frustration, suffering, or bereavement. At a higher level, the influence of mechanistic views in Biology and Physics and behaviourist ideas in Psychology has been to deprive men of a sense of responsibility and to destroy the consciousness of sin. The evil that men do is lightly explained away in terms of biological necessity or psychological maladjustment. What our forefathers plainly called sin we now call by fancy names that make it sound much less reprehensible; and the clinics of the psychiatrist are thronged with frustrated people who are troubled because they "do not feel well", but are quite unaware that they are actually starving. The danger is lest the soul "should persuade itself that it is not hungry". The food for which they are really hungering, beneath the sedative effects of these insidious drugs, is God's forgiveness and a purpose to live for.

This then is the intellectual and spiritual climate in which our children are growing up; and as we watch them becoming more and more engrossed in the mechanical excitements of jet aircraft, rockets, atomic warfare, and the imagined prospects of inter-planetary travel, we may well wonder whether the next generation may find an even more empty and spurious fulfilment than ours has done in dreams of scientific conquest. But it is interesting to notice that serious writers about the Future are no longer tempted to depict it as a Golden Age. Utopian dreams have given place to a whole sequence of gruesome nightmares—*Brave New World, Ape and Essence, 1984, That Hideous*

Strength, these are the kind of pictures that haunt the minds of thinking men as they try to forecast the future of a technological civilization that has largely lost its sanctions and its sense of purpose. Behind the impressive façade of scientific power and achievement, man's spiritual nature remains unaltered. He is still actuated by motives of self-will and at the mercy of primitive impulses of pride, anger, lust, envy, covetousness, greed, and indolence. He is still in fact self-centred. To put untold power into the hands of unredeemed men, whatever their brilliance as scientists and technicians, is like handing round loaded revolvers to a crowd of children in a nursery school. It is only when they become responsible beings that they can safely be entrusted with such power.

What does it mean to become responsible beings? "Responsible" means "answerable" or "accountable"; and in the last resort there is only one supreme authority to whom all men are answerable—and that is God. Man is accountable to God for *everything*. If this is God's world and the arena in which God's plans and purposes are being worked out, then clearly there is not a single thing in it which is outside the scope of God's concern. The whole Universe is God's business and, in a sense, nobody else's. It is only by taking account of God's will at every juncture that man can hope to keep his life in conformity with "the grain of the Universe" and find the peace and fulfilment he craves for. All the strains and stresses from which men suffer arise from their vain efforts to run the world contrary to the spiritual laws which God has imposed upon them. The evidence of two world wars and the increasing tensions of the Atomic Age should be enough to convince anyone that we have been following the wrong road; but even our uneasiness on this score is liable to be infected by our incurable self-assurance. As Professor Jeffreys has reminded us, modern man "clings in desperation to the

3

dogma of human self-sufficiency, and thus paradoxically combines increasing uneasiness about the state of civilization with an obstinate complacency about Man".[1]

The Christian answer to this dilemma is the same as it has always been. Although the material setting of man's life has changed more in the last half-century (even in the last decade) than in all the previous ages of history put together, man himself, divested of his glittering playthings, is still "an infant crying in the dark". He still needs God and cannot live without him; because that is how God made him and no amount of technological achievement can ever alter that simple fact. "Thou, O God, hast made us for thyself, and our hearts are restless till they rest in thee", cried St Augustine of Hippo. "The chief end of man is to glorify God and enjoy him for ever", says the Shorter Catechism—and that note of "enjoyment" is one we need to emphasize a great deal more. People too readily think of God as a kind of Almighty Clergyman (if not an Almighty Policeman) and their pictures of Heaven make it seem like an everlasting Church Service! Those are childish pictures, on a level with crude medieval conceptions of heaven and hell. All the finest and most satisfying experiences we know are merely broken glimpses of the supreme bliss that the vision of God will afford—the most complete satisfaction of all our hunger. How are we to find our way to this fulfilment which is God's purpose for all of us? The answer is —through *Worship*; and the rest of this book is an effort to substantiate that surprising claim. Man has been described as a "worshipping animal"—and worship is as essential to his eternal wellbeing (and to his wellbeing in this world also) as food is to the health of his body. Without worship he will starve and perish.

This is not an easy message to convey to practical-minded

[1] Professor M. V. C. Jeffreys, *Glaucon: An Enquiry into the Aims of Education* (Pitmans), p. 114.

4

and self-sufficient modern man, drugged by the spectacular triumphs of technology. There are indeed signs that his armour has already been pierced by the disillusionment with science caused by the prospect of atomic warfare, and that he may be increasingly disposed to listen again to the Christian Good News. But meanwhile, if we are given time, our main hope lies with the children not yet contaminated by the false values and standards that prevail in our western civilization. That is why the chief emphasis of this book is on the training of our children in the life of worship.

Chief emphasis of Book to ...

But, I must hasten to add, this does not mean that this is an elementary and superficial treatment of the subject. On the contrary, it is my own firm conviction that only those who have a deep and penetrating grasp of any matter are suitably equipped to communicate it to the acute perception of children. For that reason I urge that the book should be studied as a whole. It is intended to help parents, teachers, clergy, and all others who try to lead children in the way of religion, and you may be tempted to study only the chapters that seem to have a bearing on your own particular problems and skip the rest! That would be a pity; because the whole thing hangs together as an organic unity, and the more intimate problems of home life are inextricably interwoven with the problems of Church and School. The future of religious education must be a close partnership between parent, priest, and teacher, and we need to be acquainted with each others' peculiar problems and the means available for handling them. Above all, I beg that you will pay careful attention to the four opening chapters, in which I have attempted to give a *rationale* of Worship and Prayer without which our approach to "practical difficulties" is liable to be superficial and ineffective. It is my hope that these chapters may also serve as an introduction to worship which may prove comprehensible and relevant to many thoughtful readers who have allowed their faith to be sapped by the "acids of modernity".

I must express my indebtedness to the Rev. A. W. Hastings, Editor of the *Expository Times*, for permission to expand the substance of several articles he invited me to contribute to that journal; to the B.B.C. for allowing me to reproduce some material originally written for broadcasting; and to my friend, the Bishop of Warrington, for kindly adding, in a Foreword, the weight of his knowledge and authority to these concerns which we have so often discussed together.

JOHN G. WILLIAMS

St Columba's, Anfield
  Liverpool
    Advent, 1956

I

What is Worship?

A MAN, with very little knowledge of the scientific principles involved, might ask the question: "How does an aircraft become airborne?" He might go on to say: "Please give me a very brief answer in words of one syllable." What sort of reply could be given to such a question? Obviously the man might be taught to fly an aircraft and to manipulate the controls, without ever grasping the many complex problems of aerodynamics involved at every point; but if he really wants to understand *why* he is required to do certain things and *how* those things achieve the effect of keeping the aeroplane in flight, then he must be prepared to study the basic principles. He will need to know about the nature of the internal-combustion engine or the jet; about the structure of the aircraft and its controls; about the laws governing the motion of air and their mechanical effects. It is only within the setting of such a comprehensive knowledge that he can hope for a "simple" answer to his practical question. In fact, once he begins to grasp the underlying principles the questions answer themselves.

People often ask this kind of question, requiring a simple reply, about practical problems of Religion—especially about Prayer and Worship. It is often possible to give some brief and practical reply which simple folk may find reasonably satisfying. But no answer can be completely satisfactory, specially to more searching minds, unless it takes fundamental principles into account; and once the basic principles are acknowledged the problems tend to answer themselves.

For that reason, in talking to teachers and parents about

such problems as children's prayers or the conducting of school worship, I have always begun by trying to give a fairly comprehensive sketch of the deep-seated theological truths underlying worship; and in my experience this kind of approach has often forestalled and illuminated the questions people most wanted to ask. Time and time again a questioner has remarked "What you said about the nature of worship and its laws has already answered my point." That is why I shall make no apology for beginning this book about the problems of training children in prayer and worship by offering a fairly stiff (though I hope not unnecessarily complex) introduction to the theology of worship.

A Definition of Worship

What, then, do we mean by worship? The word itself is derived from the Anglo-Saxon word *weorthscipe*—"worth-ship". It means, for a person, the condition of being held in honour and esteem. The stress is on the idea of "worth" or "value" or "personal merit". We use the word in several derived senses—"His Worship the Mayor", "The Worshipful Company of Haberdashers" and, in the Marriage Service, "with my body I thee worship"—but always with this overriding idea of recognizing personal worth and esteem and giving honour. So to "worship" anything (or anybody) is quite simply to acknowledge the value it possesses for us. It means to treat that person or thing as wholly worth while, so that it becomes for us what the psychologist calls a "master-sentiment". This is bound to have very practical results, because whatever we consider as wholly worth while will colour our attitude to everything else and dominate our thoughts and our activities. The miser worships money. The dictator worships power. The libertine worships sexual gratification. The lover worships the beloved. In all these cases the object of worship inspires

8

an <u>all-consuming passion</u> <u>to which every other consideration</u> <u>is made subservient</u>. The danger of allowing our worship to become attached to transient and "creaturely" things is at once apparent. Those things may pass away at any moment and leave us bereaved and frustrated. The Christian knows that the only true and enduring object of such worship is God. So the word "worship" is in general reserved for the honour, the respect, the acknowledgment of supreme worth, given to God alone.

The best definition of worship I have ever come across (though I cannot now remember the source) is this: "*Wor-ship is the all-pervading recognition of the absolute worth of God.*" Look at it in detail. "All-pervading" reminds us that the worship of God is concerned with <u>life at every point</u>. There is no part of life that is not comprehended by true worship. It is indeed a "master-sentiment". It may be compared with "falling in love", which is far and away the best analogy on the purely human level. For a man in love there is no doubt what is the one object that possesses all his thoughts and determines all his activities. This complete and constant obsession with the loved one gives him a new pride and purpose in his work; it inflames him with a desire to be his best in everything; to please, honour, and serve the beloved. It takes hold of his whole life and becomes a driving-force that overcomes every obstacle. There is no single aspect of his daily life, however trivial, that is not touched and empowered and enriched by it. That is a glimpse of what it means to worship God. There is a sense in which Religion means being in love with God. In fact, much of the language of adoration remains cold and meaningless till we realize that. We ought to recognize all the finest and most satisfying experiences of life as being glimpses of God and of Heaven. Once see God as the one truly "worth-while" object of all our thoughts, love, and energy and then every conceivable detail of life—home,

9

work, recreations, friendships, aims, and ideals—will be permeated by one all-embracing purpose, to please and honour God. God will be seen (as indeed he is, whether we see it or not) as the heart and core of all things. That is what "all-pervading" means.

2. Then "recognition". In its fullest meaning "recognition" is an activity of the whole personality—not just of the mind, but also of the emotions and of the will. For example, I "recognize" the Law of England first by knowing it, then by respecting it, and finally by obeying it. So with my "recognition" of God. It begins with knowing him, as he has revealed his nature and purpose in Jesus Christ; that passes into respect and reverence and, at its highest, love; and that in turn finds its practical outlet in obedience and a way of life. All that, as we shall see more fully in a moment, is embraced by this word "recognition". It is perfectly summarized in the Prayer of St Richard of Chichester: "... that we may *know* thee more clearly, *love* thee more dearly, and *follow* thee more nearly". So the whole of my personality is engaged in the activity of worship—intellect, affections, and will—and every response I make to the world around me with these three inseparable parts of my being is shot through with the presence of God and with concern for his honour.

Finally, notice what it is that I thus "recognize". It is
3. the "absolute worth of God". There are plenty of things in which I acknowledge worth and value. At the lowest I am bound to value the material amenities of life—food, clothing, the house I live in, the instruments of my work. At a higher level I value my home and family, my job and my friends, and especially the ones I love most dearly. We should make a desperate mistake to value any of these things too lightly; and yet, when we face the fact of change and decay and death, it is clear that all those passing things have only a temporary and subordinate value. This is one

of the most difficult lessons for those who try to live without God. All those things, however precious, we must one day relinquish; they serve a purpose only for a while. Their value is, as we say, relative—not absolute. Their purpose, if we could but see it clearly, is to lead us on to the one object of reverence and esteem which can never pass away —that is, God himself. We can only truly value these other things by seeing them as part of God and his plan for us and the world. In the last resort, the one and only purpose for which God has given me my life is that I may "love him and enjoy him for ever". I can never come to rest in any satisfaction (however noble) short of God himself. "Thou hast made us for thyself", said St Augustine, "and our hearts are restless till they rest in thee". So all the other things we value, and rightly, can only be valued at their true worth if we see them as stepping stones to God. <u>God is the one enduring rock</u> amid the swirling sea of change and dissolution, 'the eternal flux of things"; and that is what we mean by saying that he is "absolute" and everything else is "relative". "The absolute worth of God" means, then, that God's value in our estimation must be seen as something eternal and enduring that transcends the merely temporal order.

So there, to begin with, is a very comprehensive summary of what worship involves: "The all-pervading recognition of the absolute worth of God". We can now go on to consider what this means in terms of practical <u>day-to-day living</u> <u>—to reverence and honour God in all things.</u> *Pract. mng.*

This brings us to the very heart of Religion; and there are two important aspects of such worship, such giving honour to God, perfectly expressed in some phrases of the <u>General Thanksgiving</u>: ". . . that we show forth thy praise, *l.* not only with our *lips*,' but in our *lives*,' by giving up ourselves to thy service, and by walking before thee in holiness and righteousness all our days". The *worship of our lips*

means all that is included in the formal practice of Religion
—prayer, public worship, and all other verbal and ceremonial expressions of our homage. The *worship of our
lives* means everything that is embraced under the heading
of morality and ethics—the good life. "The soul of religion",
said John Bunyan, in his quaint way, "is the practic part"
—though in fact the two parts cannot be separated. Faith
and works must go hand in hand.

less faith of "lips" in sense of the hearts faith (trust, clinging God thro christ).

The Cultus and the Ethic

To simplify the distinction between these two sides of
worship, I will call the first one the *Cultus* (a word used to
denote any system of formal worship in the narrower sense)
and the second the *Ethic* (a word used to denote any system
of moral principles and rules of conduct—a code of behaviour); and, though all religions contain these two aspects,
we shall be concerned entirely with the Christian Cultus
and the Christian Ethic. These two are, in a sense, the inner
and the outer aspects of religion; the subjective and the
objective; the soul and the body. Let us look at them more
closely, beginning with the Ethic because many people find
the practical approach to religion more immediately understandable.

The Christian Ethic (the Worship of our Lives) *q. 2 c 2*

A glance at the meaning of the Christian Ethic will help
us to clear up at the outset one of the commonest misunderstandings about religion. We do in fact "worship" God—
that is recognize and acknowledge how much (or how
little) he is "worth" to us—by the very way we live. Every
detail of our life at every moment is either honouring or
dishonouring God, either proclaiming his "worth" or
obscuring it. That is a sobering thought. It means that life
is compacted of worship and sin, inextricably mixed, and
our aim as Christians must be to let the element of worship

predominate, so that we do all things to the glory of God. This simple, practical truth is often forgotten and leads to confusion. There is a real danger of regarding worship as primarily the _Cultus_—what happens in church or in the privacy of our own prayer times—unrelated to the daily concerns of ordinary life. This was a perennial problem to the Hebrews, as the great Prophets tried to wean them from a heathen morality which was not consistent with their high conception of God's nature. "They honour me with their lips, but their heart [will] is far from me" (Isa. 29.13). "Thou desirest not sacrifice, else would I give it thee; thou delightest not in burnt offerings. The sacrifices of God are a broken spirit; a broken and a contrite heart, O God, thou wilt not despise" (Ps. 51.16,17). "Bring no more vain oblations... your new moons and your appointed feasts my soul hateth: they are a trouble unto me; I am weary to bear them.... I will not hear you: your hands are full of blood. Wash you, make you clean; put away the evil of your doings from before mine eyes; cease to do evil; learn to do well; seek judgment, relieve the oppressed, judge the fatherless, plead for the widow (Isa. 1.13-17). Such quotations could be multiplied from the Old Testament writers, struggling against a situation in which the Cultus was divorced from the Ethic, a system of religious observances that had no bearing on moral conduct.

In true worship Cultus and Ethic cannot be thus divorced. They are two sides of the same coin. Every single detail of our personal and social life must be ordered in a way that "worships" God, that is, acknowledges and proclaims his infinite worth. I say "acknowledges and proclaims", because the quality of my moral life is an act of worship affecting both me and other people; it represents my own recognition of God's supremacy, but it also helps other people to recognize him too. "Let your light so shine before men that they may see your good works and glorify your

13

Father which is in heaven" (Matt. 5.16). That is a terribly searching principle. I can apply it at once to every item of my life—my home, my friendships, my business deals, my pleasures, my attitude towards other people (especially my enemies), my social responsibilities and political affiliations, my plans and ideals, my pet aversions and prejudices. Do these things honour and reflect God—or do they dishonour and obscure him? In the same way we may ask, Does the ordering of our society honour God or dishonour him? Does it, for example, acknowledge and proclaim the truth of God's Fatherhood? (I suggest that the chief reason why our generation has largely lost the sense of God is because for over a hundred years our whole social system, with its slums and unemployment, its industrial strife and internecine war, has been a bleak denial of all that Christians hold God to be. Our basic assumptions have been essentially self-centred and atheistic.)

This is God's World. He made it, and it is his purpose that is being worked out in it. Therefore nothing in the whole world can possibly be outside the range of his concern, from my own most private thoughts and aspirations to the sort of comity of nations that we hope to build out of the present disorder. Everything must honour God and hallow his name; the sphere of worship is coterminous with the entire Universe and everything it contains. That then is the worship of our lives, the Christian Ethic.

But here we must take careful note of a further complication which sometimes obscures religious truth. The ordinary man-in-the-street does in fact tend to regard what he calls "practical religion" as simply a matter of "living a decent life" according to a very simple code of decency. To him religion is just a matter of moral conduct, and he cannot see the need for God and the Church. "I am quite as good as the people who go to church—and better than most of them", he says. (Though, in point of fact, he is not. There

14

is a desperate sickness in the human soul; and, without God, both the sanctions and the power of the Good Life are missing, as we see clearly enough when we consider the effects of two world wars, the concentration camps, the extermination camps, the threat of the H-bomb, and, on the more personal level, the serious increase in petty dishonesty, marital unfaithfulness, divorce, and juvenile crime.) There is no room for such complacency if we take an honest look at ourselves and the world. But that is the Englishman's most common attitude to religion, once expressed in the bewildering remark: "The best Christian I ever met was an atheist!" There you have, perfectly summarized, this strange idea that quality of moral life, divorced from belief and worship, is the essence of religion.

Lunt here " would "say somthing

I have tried to show that the Ethic of any religion is an inseparable part of its worship, of its whole response to God; the worship of life, as well as the worship of lips. But if it is to be true worship it must be consciously and deliberately Godward and God-honouring. It is undeniable that many people who make no claim to be Christians may, by the quality of their lives, nevertheless unwittingly honour and "worship" God—people to whom our Lord would have said, "Thou art not far from the Kingdom of God." But generally speaking a merely "upright" life is still in danger of being an intensely self-centred and self-sufficient one. It can be completely without God and come under the same condemnation as the righteousness of the Pharisees. In any true worship (as Christians understand it) God is completely central. If God is not "all-pervading", if he is only of secondary importance for me, then I am virtually an atheist, and my life (however "righteous" according to a purely ethical standard) cannot be worship. In the last resort I can only honour God by loving and obeying him, and this love and obedience will involve taking my part in

15

the work and worship of the Church which he has given us.

All this will help us to pierce through the popular fallacy of "worshipping God better in the open air". The people (sometimes called "Bluedomers") who make this facile excuse for ignoring the worship of the Church do not in fact understand the first thing about real worship. We all know the delight of the open air; but the only ones who can safely seek God in the woodlands are those who have first found him in the fellowship of other human souls. Jesus taught us to seek him first in the lives of our fellowmen (Matt. 25.35-45). You cannot find God by turning your back on your fellows. To find God only in nature is to find a cruel and pagan God who cares nothing for the sorrows and agonies of human souls. Beware of Nature worship, the oldest form of Paganism, whose symbol is human sacrifice. You must find God first in the community of redeemed souls, which is his Church, and only then may you safely seek a fuller understanding of him in the mute glories of his creation.

The Christian Cultus (the Worship of our Lips)

This brings us then to a consideration of the Christian Cultus; everything that is generally understood by worship —prayer, church-going, and all the accessories of organized religion.

Here we must look for a moment at origins. Most of our religious confusion today arises from a loss of the sense of God, partly due to the obscuring of God by a social system that fails to reflect him, partly due to material satisfactions (cinema, radio, television, and high standards of comfort) which tend to stifle the sense of need and create a false impression of wellbeing. This has been described by a modern writer as "the loss of the God-dimension". We live, as it were, in a two-dimensional world, with no upward reference. But it was not so with primitive man, whose spirit was not drugged in this way with spurious satisfactions. All religions and all worship began, in primitive man, with the growth of self-consciousness—"I" over against a world of infinite mystery. That is why Man can be called a "worshipping animal". His self-consciousness is essentially an awareness of himself over against something-other-than-himself. All other animals, as far as we can tell, are self-centred and self-sufficient and probably regard the outer world as a part of themselves. The dog and the ape, with their intelligent capacity for friendship and even a simple form of altruism, may be exceptions. We do not know for certain. But Man, as soon as he became aware of himself, became aware at the same time of a whole universe over against him, "other" than him, and was immediately confronted with "mystery". He "looks before and after"; he sees his own beginnings shrouded in mystery; he faces death with a question. He sees his little life hemmed in by two unimaginable wonders—the infinity of Time and Space —and he is filled with awe and speculation. Of course, primitive man did not argue all this as we do; he was just vaguely aware of a mysterious background to all creation and was invaded by a sense of awe, tinged with terror, in the presence of this baffling "unknown". All religion begins with this sense of awe, which Otto has called the *Numinous*, the *Mysterium Tremendum*.[1] It is in fact the first impact of God, in all his majesty and mystery, on the groping, finite mind of Man. It is at this point that man becomes a "living soul" and develops that quality of "spirit" which differentiates him from the rest of the animal world.

This element of mystery and numinous awe, this bowing down of the "creature" in the presence of something infinitely greater than himself (this "utterly other" as Otto calls it) is the essence of Cultus-worship. God still remains,

[1] Rudolf Otto, *The Idea of the Holy*.

and will ever remain, a mystery incomprehensible by our finite minds. So worship begins with a kind of inarticulate awe and wonder, and it must never be allowed to lose that quality. As Evelyn Underhill has written: "Worship is the acknowledgment of transcendence, that is to say, of a Reality independent of the worshipper, which is always more or less coloured by mystery, and which is always there first".[1] As we shall see later, we can never be "familiar" with God in the bad superficial sense. The Christian revelation enables us to approach God with astonishing love and intimacy, and for that reason some forms of Christian worship have been in danger of cheapening our regard (and especially the regard of children) for his wonder and majesty. The element of numinous awe and prostrate adoration must never be lost if worship is to remain true.

The Need for Theology

But now—the history of all religious Cultus (and especially of the Christian Cultus) is the story of a growing relationship with this mysterious God; the development of some kind of personal response to him. The nature of this relationship and response, and the nature of the Ethic, that a religion fosters will obviously depend entirely on what it conceives God to be like. The primitive, who regards God (or the gods) as tyrannical and vindictive will cower before him in terror and try to propitiate him with costly human sacrifice. He will also be cruel and vindictive in his relationships with other people. In the same way the Christian Cultus is inextricably bound up with the Christian belief about God—the Christian Faith. No one can begin to understand Christian worship without assimilating, however simply, at least the elements of Christian theology. The core of worship is belief. Our fundamental Christian conviction (a matter of history, and not just a piece of pious

[1] Evelyn Underhill, *Worship*.

18

guesswork) is that God has torn the veil from the mystery of his own being and revealed himself, within the limits of our finite understanding, in the person of Jesus Christ, true God and true Man. Above and beyond that, he still remains great and mysterious beyond our comprehension, but his essential nature (his righteousness, power, justice, and love) has been expressed in terms of a human life. When we go on to enquire *why* God did this incredible thing, we find ourselves plunged into the theology of Sin and Redemption, of Grace and Sacrament. In the next chapter we will develop a little further this great system of Christian theology which is briefly summarized in the historic creeds. For the moment it is my purpose only to point out that in all that body of revealed truth about God and the world, Christian worship (both Ethic and Cultus) is firmly rooted. You cannot have Christianity without Christian belief and without the Christian Church. So at the very heart and core of all Christian worship there lies Christian "dogma". That is an unpopular word, so it is best to be clear about what it means. Dogma means, strictly, "revealed truth", truth that we know because God himself has chosen to give it to us. (It is not to be confused with "doctrine" which is the attempt to express this basic truth in the current language of a particular age. Fashions in doctrine may change and the language of doctrine may become outworn; but the Faith "once delivered to the saints" remains the unshaken rock on which the whole Christian way of life and worship is built.) These truths, I repeat, crisply stated in the Creeds, represent, not wistful hopes or inspired guesses or pious opinions, but truths of fact that God himself has laid bare to us.

So it is quite imperative that the outward forms of Christian worship (the Cultus) should be soundly based in these dogmatic truths of the Faith and should be constantly confronting us with them. Christian worship has nothing in common with the airy aspirations and sentimental "uplift" that sometimes pass for devotion—"the mist of pious verbiage" that titillates the emotions without challenging the mind or the will. All the liturgies of Christendom are saturated through and through with dogmatic truth, bracing and austere, confronting us at every step with what God has shown us of himself, with what God has done, and his purpose for the world through Christ and his Church.

Belief the Foundation of Worship

So, to summarize, the Christian Ethic and the Christian Cultus, closely linked with each other, are indissolubly wedded to Christian Belief. This is absolutely fundamental, and to grasp this truth is to solve in a flash many of the perplexing problems with which the day-to-day practice of religion (and not least the training of our children), constantly faces us. My moral conduct and sort of worship I offer God (and they belong together) will be entirely determined by what I believe God to be like. This is the truth behind the old Latin tag *Lex orandi, lex credendi*. The law of worship is the law of belief. They are one and the same thing.

So the first step towards true Christian worship (both of our lips and of our lives) is the acceptance of the Christian Faith. Beware of that pernicious idea, so commonly expressed by the Englishman, "It doesn't matter what a man believes as long as he lives a good life." That is really quite poisonous nonsense, as has been amply demonstrated in our own age by the Nazi and Communist movements, as well as by the blank *laisser-faire* attitude of the ordinary unbelieving pagan. Everything depends on what you believe —or refuse to believe. My whole attitude to God and other people and the world at large derives precisely from what I believe. And here I may again offer the reminder that what I really believe is that which prompts me to action. Many people repeat the Creed on Sundays and give lip-service to Christian belief, and yet live the rest of the week as if God did not exist. "They worship me with their lips but their heart is far from me." That is effective atheism, and it is not surprising that their lives demonstrate the kind of godlessness which brings the Church into disrepute. That is perfectly consonant with what I have been saying and precisely what one would expect. It underlines very powerfully the thought with which I shall conclude this brief survey of the principles of Christian worship—it is only when I *believe* rightly that I can *live* rightly, and it is only when I live rightly that I can *worship* rightly.

2

The Worship of the Church

Summary chap I WE saw in the last chapter how, in its fullest sense, worship means honouring God—acknowledging and proclaiming God's infinite worth—by the whole disposition of life in every detail. The Cultus and the Ethic are inseparably linked, and most of our confusions about religion are due to an attempt to divorce them.

Then we considered how, as in all religions, the Cultus and the Ethic of Christianity are quite inseparable from Faith—what you believe about God and the world at large. What you think God is like will obviously determine how you think you can best honour and serve him. So, at the core of all our worship, there lies the whole system of Christian dogma, of revealed truth about God and his activity in the world; and, to anyone who is not prepared to accept the Faith as absolutely central, the activity of prayer and worship (the Christian Cultus) will remain meaningless, and even nonsensical. But it cannot be watered down and adapted to suit unbelieving minds; though this is sometimes attempted in "popular" types of service, and even Prayer Book Revision has not been free from this danger. It is one against which we need to be constantly on our guard.

Summary of Christian Belief

It might be valuable to pause here for a moment and remind ourselves briefly of the fundamental Christian beliefs, summed up in the historic creeds, without which the Christian Cultus is bound to be unacceptable and even offensive. The modern tendency to dilute the Christian religion and to accommodate its forms of worship to the sensitivities of people who are not ready to accept it derives largely from the fact that the doctrine of sin and man's need of grace is offensive to twentieth-century pride and self-sufficiency. But the essence of Christian belief is that God made man for eternal fellowship with himself, without which man will always remain frustrated and unfulfilled; that man has become separated from God by an insidious force in the world called sin; that man is himself unable to break the bondage of sin and set himself free, and that God has therefore taken the initiative and provided a means of release and restoration. He did this by himself becoming a man in Christ and entering the human arena of sin and conflict, creating a new level of human life ("the perfect man"—the last stage in the evolution of humanity) which is absolutely one with the life of God. "God was in Christ reconciling the world unto himself" (2 Cor. 5.19). This new life, the life of Christ, is now imparted to man through the medium of the divine Society, the Church, and especially in the Sacraments. By this means the power of sin can be broken, the life of God released in us, and man can be restored to that unhindered fellowship with God which is his destiny. "The chief end of man is to glorify God and enjoy him for ever." This is the merest summary, but it covers the whole field. Everything else in the Christian Cultus and Ethic hangs upon those basic truths. Apart from them, Christian worship is unintelligible and may even appear ridiculous.

All the practical problems we shall be considering later, as we think of ways of introducing our children to the activity of worship, will be illuminated if we can get a clear grasp of this conception; and so it will clarify our whole approach to the Christian Cultus if we look at the origin and development of it. This is no more than a brief

WORSHIP AND THE MODERN CHILD

sketch, but it will serve our purpose; and if it appears to be rather over-simplified I ask your forgiveness. In broad outline it is a true picture.

B. *The Idea of Atonement*

It is a belief common to all religions that the gods require a certain standard of behaviour from their devotees (the Ethic). This standard, specially in primitive religions, is not always what we should regard as a highly moral one. In the early stages of religion it often consists of little more than the observance of all kinds of apparently amoral or neutral *taboos*, together with positive activities which may even, according to our standards, involve immorality. The point to notice is that the devotees of these religions believe that the gods do in fact require this kind of behaviour from them and that any infringement is therefore an offence against the gods. In higher forms of religion this system of observances will consist of certain ethical standards which must be kept. But in either case the belief is that any violation of these requirements (Ethic) is an offence incurring the displeasure and vengeance of the gods; and the Cultus of every religion has always consisted largely of ritual and ceremonial means whereby atonement can be made and the gods propitiated. However crude this may appear, you see here the germ of the belief (fully in accord with Christian doctrine) that "sin", taken in its widest sense, separates from God and that something must be done to repair the breach and effect reconciliation. In all religions that "something" has consisted primarily in the offering of sacrifices by priests.

Let us look more carefully at the whole idea of Priests and Sacrifices.

C. *The Priest*

What is the chief purpose of the Priest in any religious

24

system? Broadly speaking, he is the man who is appointed *1. Purpose*
to act as a mediator between God and man. A mediator is
one who brings together and reconciles two people who
have become estranged. You see how, ideally, a mediator
"stands between", not to separate, but to bring together. A
man engaged in reconciling two enemies or introducing
two strangers may stand between them for a moment, but
his purpose is not to keep them apart but to effect a union
between them. (It is worth bearing this truth in mind when
you hear people say, as they do quite commonly about the
Sacrament of Penance, "I will never allow a priest to stand
between my soul and God.") Man has become estranged
from God and needs to be reconciled; and the thing that
causes this estrangement is sin. So it has always been one *2. function*
of the chief functions of the priest to deal with sin, to make
atonement for the sins of the people. How did all primitive
priests deal with sin and attempt to effect reconciliation?
By means of *sacrifices*. "For every high priest taken from
among men is ordained for men in things pertaining to
God, that he may offer both gifts and sacrifices for sins"
(Heb. 5.1). We shall therefore have to spend a little time
trying to grasp the meaning of "sacrifice".

D. *Sacrifice*

Even the most primitive savages offer sacrifices to their
gods; and, as we have seen, they are prompted by the
belief that the gods are offended by their "sin", even if that
sin is no more than the unconscious infringement of a
taboo, and must be propitiated by the offering of something
really costly. All sacrifice is costly. The word is meaning- *1.*
less, even in our more general modern use of it, if the
idea of sacrificial cost is excluded. In most of the early
forms of religion you will find the custom of offering
human sacrifice. Don't misunderstand it. The primitive
believes that if the gods are to be appeased they demand an

offering of tremendous value; and we can well imagine the feelings of a mother as she watched her child being passed through the fires to Moloch or mangled on the altars of Stonehenge. It is a mistake to regard such sacrifices as merely savage and brutal. They were, mistaken as they might be, the offering of a terribly precious gift.

The ancient Hebrews began too with the offering of human sacrifice, and the heart-breaking cost of it is made very clear in the story of Abraham and Isaac (Gen. 22). But this story is also the account of a great advance in religious understanding, because (into the Semitic world where human sacrifice was an almost universal practice) came the assurance that God does not desire it, and the ram was substituted for the boy. But the Hebrews still felt the need of offering God some gift of great value as a recompense for sin; and so there developed the Old Testament system of animal sacrifices which persisted right down to the time of our Lord. But notice carefully the overriding requirement in the animal sacrifices. Whatever animal was offered, whether it was a costly bullock or only a pair of sparrows, it must be the best and most perfect they could provide, without spot or blemish. "Your lamb shall be without blemish" (Ex. 12.5). A creature that was diseased or crippled was no fit offering at God's altar.

The Perfect Sacrifice

Now all these crude and primitive ideas contain a profound and indestructible truth. They represent a groping after the real thing. The Hebrews realized that in order to merit God's forgiveness they must be prepared to offer him something of tremendous value and as perfect as it could possibly be. It was to be some compensation for the imperfection of their own tainted lives. But, as we have seen, they were still in danger of treating these sacrifices very lightly. They were not as troubled as they ought to have

26

been about the evil of their ways and were all too ready
to imagine that everything could be put right by this simple
expedient of animal sacrifice. Throughout the Old Testament (as we considered in the last chapter) we find count-
less passages in which God, through the mouth of psalmist
or prophet, made it quite clear that he requires, not the
blood of bulls or goats, however perfect, but a life of goodness, justice, and obedience. Throughout the whole of their
troubled history the Hebrew people were being constantly
confronted with this challenge, but even in the time of our
Lord only very few of them had come to accept it. Our
Lord's denunciation of the Scribes and Pharisees is the
indictment of a Cultus still divorced from the Ethic. "Woe
unto you, Scribes and Pharisees, hypocrites ... for ye outwardly appear righteous unto men, but within ye are full
of hypocrisy and iniquity" (Matt. 23.28).

God requires not merely a good life but a perfect life.
"Be ye therefore perfect", said our Lord, "even as your
Father which is in heaven is perfect" (Matt. 5.48). But
what an impossible demand! We might offer the sacrifice
of a reasonably perfect lamb or bullock, but the sacrifice of
a perfect human life—that is outside the bounds of possibility! So we are tempted to think, until we look again at
the Christian Gospel and realize that the impossible has
actually been done. The truth about what God really
requires—the truth after which all the religions of the
world have blindly groped and of which all have been
broken glimpses—is clearly revealed in the only perfect
sacrifice for sin that has ever been offered, the sacrifice of
Christ on the cross of Calvary. We shall never fully understand the meaning and power of our Lord's *death* until
we see it as the climax and fulfilment of a *life* wholly given
and dedicated to God down to the last detail; a life without spot or blemish; a life of absolute perfection. "He was
in all points tempted like as we are, yet *without sin*" (Heb.

27

4.15). The life of Christ was from beginning to end an act of unbroken "worship"; and when on the cross, in the face of all the hostile forces of evil and pain that sought to break him, our Lord yielded that life into the hands of the Father, he offered to God the sacrifice of the first and only human life that has ever been what God intended all human lives to be. When Jesus cried triumphantly, "It is finished!" (or, as we might better translate the words, "It is achieved!") God looked down from Heaven on the first and only human life that has ever been wholly given to him. For the first time in the history of the world, Perfect Man had come into being. So the Hebrews, as they offered God their lambs and bullocks, were quite right when they guessed that God required of them a perfect sacrifice. All this helps us to understand why one of our Lord's most honoured titles is "The Lamb of God that taketh away the sin of the world".

"In Christ"

But how (we go on to ask) can even that perfect sacrifice do away our sin and bring us back into fellowship with God? The answer to that question brings us to the inner heart of all Christian worship, the point where the Ethic and the Cultus meet. What God requires of us is absolute perfection—perfect love and obedience to him, perfect love and concern for our fellow-men. But our lives are already deeply tainted with sin and self-will; and even if from this moment onwards we could offer God the rest of our days quite free from failure, the past is already indelibly corrupted. There is no hope that any of us can offer him the sacrifice of an unblemished life. And this is where God himself has come to meet our desperate need. To put it at its simplest, that perfect human life of Christ, released in death, "risen, ascended, glorified", and now for ever joined with the perfect Being of God himself, can come and take possession of us and transform us from within. That, and nothing less than that, is the heart of the Christian Gospel. The whole essence of the Christian Religion, and therefore of Christian worship, is the experience of being invaded and possessed by the perfect life of Christ. It is a mystical union which St Paul denoted by the profound term ἐν Χριστῷ—"in Christ". Once grasp this truth, and it is immediately obvious that any view of religion which regards it purely as our own unaided striving after goodness or our own personal aspirations towards God is very far from Christian truth, and so are any forms of worship which express that kind of attitude. This throws a flood of light on that typically British heresy (called Pelagianism) which imagines that we can hope to offer God the Good Life he requires of us by our own human effort. That, as someone has said, is like trying to lift ourselves by our own shoe-straps. "Apart from me", said our Lord, "you can do nothing" (John 15.5); and that is the truth about our human predicament to which the whole Christian religion is the very practical answer. It is only when I am invaded and possessed by the spirit of Christ, by that "divine indwelling", that the power of my evil will can be broken and the life of God can begin to shape my life according to his purpose. That is the practical truth that underlies the Christian conception of "rebirth"—"Ye must be born again" (John 3.7). "If any man be *in Christ* he is a new creature" (2 Cor. 5.17). "My little children, of whom I am again in travail until Christ be formed in you..." (Gal. 4.19). When the perfect life of Christ, poured out in sacrifice on Calvary, comes to reinforce my own feeble struggles after goodness, then my weakness can be changed into strength, my cowardice into courage, my defeat into victory. "I can do all things through Christ who strengthens me" (Phil. 4.13). We may therefore picture Christian experience as a kind of blood-transfusion, an inoculation of clean and perfect life into our tainted souls.

The Necessity of the Church

But this is not a purely personal and private matter. Religion has been described as "what a man does with his solitariness"—"the flight of the alone to the Alone". Many people, even professing Christians, would subscribe to this idea—but it is very far from being a Christian idea. It is true that souls must come to God one by one, and that our salvation is an intensely personal and individual matter; but that is only half of the truth. The other half is enshrined in the whole nature and purpose of the Church, the Body of Christ, the Divine Society. Jesus said, "I am the Vine: ye are the branches" (John 15.5). St Paul, developing the same idea with a different metaphor, wrote: "Ye are the body of Christ, and members in particular" (1 Cor. 12.27). Although God loves each one of us separately and individually, yet our individual isolation is largely illusory. We are all "members one of another". We are each separate twigs on the tree of Humanity and yet inseparably wedded to the tree. That is why, because the tree of Humanity is a tainted tree, we all share in the taint; just as a diseased apple-tree will bear diseased apples, even though the apples themselves might disclaim any responsibility for their share in the disease! This analogy illuminates the doctrine of Original Sin. It also throws a great deal of light on the nature of the Church—the perfect Vine, of which the Life, permeating every branch to the remotest twig, is the perfect life of Christ himself; and it is into this Vine that we are "grafted" by our Baptism so that the life of Christ may flow into us. But it is a life that we share in common with all the other branches of the vine, all the other limbs of the Body of Christ. We will look more fully at this in a moment.

But first, consider what happens when a man has this

essential Christian experience of being "in Christ", because it will help us to understand how the perfect sacrifice on Calvary avails to take away the sin of the world. When my life is in that way, in spite of all its present sin and imperfection, united with the perfect life of Christ, two things happen. First, God is able to accept and forgive me as if I were already perfect. Righteousness is "imputed" to me, not because I yet possess it, but because with Christ's help I have set myself in the way of possessing it. That is called *Justification*. Secondly, by this "divine indwelling", all the perfection and power of Christ's own life is working in me, with my willing co-operation, to sterilize the poison of my evil will and to bring me gradually to that perfection which God intends for me; so that one day I shall be fully acceptable to God "in Christ". That is called *Sanctification*. So the breach between us and God is healed. He begins by meeting us more than half-way, still in our sins, and then slowly leads us on to perfection. But no part of the process is possible until I am "in Christ". God can only thus accept and enable me in so far as I am united with the perfect life of Christ, offering myself to him in union with that only complete self-offering, the sacrifice of Christ. That is why merely "being good" is not enough. We cannot be accepted on our own merits alone, because we do not possess any. Our highest virtues are corrupted by self-will. God cannot be satisfied with anything less than total perfection—and it is only in Christ that we shall ever hope to acquire it. This is something of what we mean when we say that the perfect sacrifice of Christ saves us from sin and its consequences and reconciles us with God. "I am the way", said our Lord. "No man cometh unto the Father but by me" (John 14.6).

The Sacraments

We must go on now to look at the appointed means by

31

which Christ in this way imparts his perfect life to us. This
is the living heart of the Christian Cultus—the Church and
the Sacraments. By our Baptism we are grafted into the
Body of Christ. We are, so to speak, lopped off the tainted
tree of Humanity and incorporated into another tree, another organism, through which the perfect life of Christ
flows. We are "born again" of water and the Holy Spirit.
Then, just as the limbs and members of my body are under
the control of the one life that informs the body (myself),
and just as the life-giving blood is pumped to the most
remote and insignificant parts; so, within the Body of
Christ, every "member" is under the control of the one
spirit, Christ himself; and the veins and arteries through
which his life-giving power is brought to us are the sacraments. In the sacraments God uses common material things
—the water of Baptism, the bread and wine of Holy Communion, the words of Absolution, and so on—as vehicles
through which his spiritual gifts of forgiveness and strength
—in fact his very life—may pass into our souls. Every sacrament is the "outward and visible sign of an inward and
spiritual grace." It is both the vehicle and also the material
evidence and assurance of a spiritual event which might
otherwise remain uncertain; "a means whereby we receive
the same and a pledge to assure us thereof".[1]

So God imparts to us the perfect life of Christ through
the sacramental life of his Church, though the full grace
of the Sacraments can only be appropriated and assimilated
by our own personal life of prayer and self-offering. This
brings us to the very heart of the matter and the inner core
of the Christian Worship, which is essentially the "union
which is betwixt Christ and his Church"; the whole process
of being caught up into the life of God and made one with
him. The central focus of Christian worship, from which
all else radiates, is the act of "communion", represented in

[1] The Catechism.

the Christian Cultus by the Sacrament of Holy Communion itself, instituted by Christ and obediently observed (with only one or two exceptions) by all his followers. Whether it be the Mass (with its high doctrine of the real and corporeal presence of Christ) or whether it be the simplest "breaking of bread" round the Lord's table (based upon a simple doctrine of Memorial) all Christian worship in the last resort derives its meaning from that mysterious union of the soul with God, through Christ, by which the entail of sin is broken in us and we are enabled to offer God perfect honour. You see how entirely impossible it is for worship to be conceived in terms of emotional uplift, divorced from theology, or scaled down to suit the tastes of nice-minded unbelievers. It is all this—or nothing.

The Offering of Christ

Christ is our great High Priest (Heb. 4.14). He has offered, and is still offering, to God the only perfect sacrifice for sin—the sacrifice of his own perfect life. Christ is both Priest and Victim in the Eucharistic Feast, and every time we come to take our part in the Service of Holy Communion we join with Christ, our great High Priest, in offering and pleading before God that perfect human life, now in heaven, which is made specially present at our altars in the Holy Sacrament. We do not offer God the blood of bulls or goats or the ashes of an heifer, but we present before him the perfect life of the perfect Man who is also God. The priest at the altar is doing (in our name) exactly what Christ is doing in heaven, praying that God will accept that perfect life as a sacrifice for our sins. But the all-important point is that we *identify* ourselves with that perfect offering. That is why it is so utterly important that we should regularly make our communion. In the act of communion we are actually linked with that perfect life of Christ, we are made one with him; and so, as we offer that sacrifice, we also offer ourselves "in Christ". In union with him we offer ourselves, our souls and bodies, to be a reasonable, holy, and living sacrifice; and that is the one and only sacrifice that God can accept.

This then—and nothing less than this—is the heart of the Christian Cultus, and all lesser and derived forms of "worship" must be seen to stem from it. A true understanding of these truths will save us from many of those shallow and futile activities, man-centred, pantheistic, and sententious, which are so often provided as a substitute for Christian devotion. In the final analysis the only acceptable "worship" must find its roots and its inspiration in the worship of the Christian Community, the Church of Christ; and any other forms of worship, whatever value they may seem to possess, are only of the nature of private and personal devotion. We shall see the importance of this distinction when we go on presently to consider some of the problems of training children in prayer and worship.

3

What is Prayer?

As we saw at the beginning of our approach to the subject of Christian worship, the only satisfactory solution of the practical problems with which it continually faces us must come from a clear grasp of underlying principles. For that reason we have spent some time discussing the whole *rationale* of Christian worship, with particular emphasis on its corporate expression in the Cultus. But we now need to give some attention to that more intimate and personal side of religion which we call *Prayer*, especially as this is the point at which the child's first approach to God is bound to begin. Most of the practical difficulties we find, as well as the mistakes we are likely to make, will be strongly illuminated and largely resolved by seeing them within the setting of a clear conception of the meaning and purpose of Prayer.

C.T.

A. The Need for Prayer

There are some very challenging statements at the beginning of Bede Frost's classic book *The Art of Mental Prayer*. "Faith, Cultus, and Sacraments", he writes, "need a background and reinforcing power. That background, that power, is the interior life of prayer. For it is prayer alone which makes the grace of the Sacraments operative in our lives. For, although the grace of the Sacraments is given *ex opere operato*, it does not produce fruit without our moral assimilation and response. This is one reason why all the masters of the spiritual life teach that mental prayer is wholly necessary to the acquiring and maintaining of even

N.B.
Lamb.

35

a low degree of holiness. We see people going regularly to Mass and the Sacraments for years, yet remaining in a mediocre and barren piety. It is because they do not really pray.... The reform and sanctification of clergy, religious, and laity all depend upon this: to pray and to teach souls to pray—it is all. For, given this, everything else will follow. The average priest and well-disposed parent imagines that if a boy or girl is brought up to say vocal prayers twice a day (and how many do even this without fail any confessor knows), is confirmed and started off with a monthly communion, it is enough. It is not enough; without mental prayer it is worth very little."[1]

I have made this extensive quotation because it sets the challenge on the very highest level. It is a challenge to our own personal religion as well as a challenge to our whole approach to children. The two go hand in hand. In the last resort children catch the practice of religion from people who themselves possess it. That is the truth behind Dean Inge's famous dictum that "religion is caught, not taught". We can never hope to take a child one step further than we have ourselves progressed. This has a powerful bearing even on the most elementary beginnings of a child's prayer life, and the more profound our own understanding and practice of prayer, the more we shall be able to guide the infant's first faltering steps without danger of misleading him or violating his growing spirit. For this reason I propose to devote this chapter to a fairly deep analysis of personal prayer, as distinct from corporate worship. As we shall see later, the young child should, ideally, grow up into a knowledge of both together from his earliest days.

Impediments to Prayer

There are two formidable enemies of the prayer life in our modern world. One is the hectic tempo of our techno-

[1] Bede Frost, *The Art of Mental Prayer* (Philip Allan).

logical civilization with all its distracting influences; the other is a deep-seated ignorance of the theology underlying *b.* Christian devotion. We will look at those first.

The chief difficulty about both learning and teaching prayer in the twentieth century is that we live in an age of perpetual noise and distraction when the last vestige of "quiet" has been banished from our life. There has never in all history been a time when it is so hard to obey the divine injunction: "Be still and know that I am God". Radio, television, the cinema, the constant roar of aircraft, the insistent demands of our high-pressure industrialism, the intensity and pace of our whole social order—these things lay constant stress on the immediate and the sensational, and the quiet things of the spirit are overwhelmed and crowded out by noise and pre-occupation. It is not so much that people no longer *believe* in God; it is rather that they are unable to "realize" God amid this tumult of pleasurable distractions. God is crowded out. It is hard not to be absorbed in the material and sensual things which dominate their whole existence. But it is impossible to apprehend God without a certain quietness, a certain deliberate opening of the spirit to his influence. Some kind of "contemplation", however rudimentary, is a pre-requisite of religious experience, and not least of prayer; and this must demand the deliberate cultivation of "silence", of waiting upon God and listening for his voice in the midst of the distractions. There is an ancient Chinese proverb: "God gave us two ears and only one mouth, so that we may listen twice as much as we speak." This is a truth that might be written large over every gateway to Prayer and Worship. "The Cathedral Builders", wrote F. R. Barry, in *The Relevance of Christianity*, "knew that the sense of the Presence could be evoked by great unfilled spaces. We have yet to learn the value, in the midst of our clamorous civilization, of unfilled intervals of time." So the first need *2 a*

37

is for a quiet, contemplative approach to God, and we must help our children also to learn this, just as they learn to walk and talk, as part of the essential equipment of their life.

2 b.   The second obstacle to prayer is the prevailing ignorance of its theological bases; and here I must be forgiven for going into some detail. In our rushing and disordered world Christians are seeking for a formula which will integrate sound thought with effective action, dogma with life. We believe that the Christian Religion, with its firm belief in the Kingship of God and the indwelling of the Holy Spirit, is the answer to all our perplexities. The problem is how to make the Faith effective in the world of affairs, whether personal or social. All true action, all effective policy, must derive from a carefully formulated and consistent philosophy of life (what the Germans call a *Weltanschauung*, a world-view). The trouble with purely man-centred Humanism is that it adopts the conclusions of the Christian Ethic without acknowledging its premisses; it plucks the fruit and denies the existence of the tree! For that reason it lacks both the necessary sanctions of the Faith and also the power that derives from it through the Holy Spirit. That is why many of us profoundly mistrust policies (like Communism) based on purely humanitarian considerations. Such movements (we acknowledge) possess much of the rich heritage of Christian thought on the manward side, but they lack belief in the ultimate meaning and purpose of Man as part of a divine plan, of which the goal lies outside the limits of the material world; a belief which alone can give value and dignity to individual human souls.

Today, therefore, we are in danger of esteeming action higher than thought or contemplation. It is the "man who gets things done", the Man with the Programme, who is likely to get a hearing and a following (like Hitler) no matter how ill-digested and even ridiculous his basic principles may be. But the only action that is worth anything, or that can achieve any lasting good, is action founded on a sound faith, a clear understanding of God and his purpose in the world (whether for the individual or for the race), kept all the time in close touch with God, the only source of effective power, through the activity of Prayer. As Evelyn Underhill has said: "All effective action issues from contemplation."

This truth, that right action can proceed only from right belief, and from a right response to God through worship, 2 b. covers the whole field of human life, personal and social. At the moment we are concerned with the personal aspect, illustrated in the activity of prayer; that part of the religious life which Plotinus described as "the flight of the alone to the Alone"; and this serves to underline again the fundamental truth that prayer itself, the most important activity of the Christian, must be firmly rooted in sound theology. It is at this point that we so often conspicuously fail. We pray badly—or do we not pray at all—because we are not at heart convinced of the theological truths which can alone make prayer a reasonable and attractive activity.

Theological Bases of Prayer C. N. B.

What are these truths? I suggest there are four outstanding ones which throw a strong light on the meaning and purpose of prayer.

(1) The first is the belief, so powerfully stated by the ancient Psalmist: "The Lord is King, be the people never so impatient; he sitteth between the cherubims, be the earth never so unquiet" (Ps. 99.1). God is the creator, sustainer, and sole ruler of the entire universe. There is nothing throughout the whole gamut of existence which is outside either the interest or the control of God. The Kingship of God is a fact, whether we know and recognize it or not, and however turbulent the world may seem. It is only by

God's continuing concern and ceaseless output of power that the world is held in being at all. "In him we live and move and have our being" (Acts 17.28).

c. 2.　　(2) The second truth underlying prayer is that God, by granting to the higher orders of his creatures a spirit "in his own image", involving complete freedom of thought, feeling, and will, has thereby limited his own immediate impact on the world. This is a serious stumbling-block to uninstructed people. They cannot understand how God can be King and yet permit, without any apparent interference, the ravages of evil so obviously opposed to his will. A quite common remark at the beginning of the last war was, "Why doesn't God strike down Hitler?" The simple answer is that, if God were to assert his Kingship by striking down those who oppose his will, there is no apparent reason why he shouldn't begin with me—and you! By giving all of us this freedom of choice he has willingly accepted the consequences; and so must we.

c 3.　　(3) The third truth derives from the second. It is that God, in working out his purpose in creation, seeks the love and willing co-operation of his higher creatures. The highest spiritual activity of which we are capable (because we are made in God's image) is Love, and it is not surprising that the one and only purpose of our existence is that we may love God and enjoy fellowship with him for ever. But all the activities of spirit (of which love is the supreme expression) can only be real when they are totally free and spontaneous. For example, I cannot say "Love me, or I'll shoot you!" I cannot say "Believe the truth or die!"—"Be good at your peril!"—"Enjoy the music of Bartok and the pictures of Van Gogh, or perish!" No idea of pressure or compulsion can be admitted in the realm of spiritual appreciation and response. Love—with its accompanying response to truth, goodness, and beauty—can only be won and spontaneously given. So God is seeking all the time to win us—and one of the chief purposes of prayer is that we may place ourselves so deliberately under the influence and attraction of God that a relationship of perfect love and co-operation can grow up between us. This gives us a clue to that doctrine unique in the Christian Religion, the doctrine of the Holy Spirit, which teaches us that God himself inhabits and informs the life of individual souls, winning their love and response, and through them works out in ever-widening circles on to the world at large. This is the function of the Church, the Spirit-bearing Body, and prayer is the process by which this miracle happens. The world is saved by God *through man*—through you and me and the whole Catholic Church; and by means of prayer my words and activities become in effect the very words and activities of God himself. I become a living point at which the power of God can touch and influence the life of the world and make his Kingship effectual. That is what "Thy Kingdom come on earth as it is in Heaven" really means.

(4) The fourth theological truth underlying prayer—and following naturally from these other three—is that nothing in the whole Universe can ever be properly understood or safely handled unless it is understood and handled in relation to God, whose world it is and whose plan is paramount throughout. Therefore (as we have already considered) there is no policy of action in any department of life, individual or corporate, which can ever be truly effective (or even safe) unless it enquires at every point: How and where does God's purpose enter into this? In brief, God lies at the very heart of our problems, whether practical or speculative, and to ignore him is obviously to ignore the most important factor in the calculation. That is the road to disaster, as we see so plainly to our cost in the disorder of human lives and the chaos of the world. This emphasizes again, as we have so often said, the absolute need of a clear

and consistent theology; that is, an understanding of what God is like in his essential nature and the purpose he is pursuing in the order of creation. The Christian Religion is the one final answer to these questions, possessing all the force and sanction of divine revelation. This links the personal activity of prayer with all the principles of faith and practice which we considered in the previous chapters. Prayer, in brief, is the means by which the Kingship of God is made actual in our life; submitting ourselves to the complete possession and guidance of God, through the indwelling Holy Spirit, so that through us God can win the whole world to himself. At every point it faces us with the absolute priority of God in all things.

D. *The Priority of God*

Another quotation from Bede Frost summarizes this whole truth perfectly. "The fundamental weakness of Christian life today", he writes, "is largely due to the fact that we are more concerned with self than with God; with the question of saving our souls rather than adoring, praising, and serving God; with fighting temptations rather than seeking God; a 'Glory for me' rather than a 'Glory be to God' religion. We do not think enough, contemplate enough, adore enough, *God in himself*. Our minds are so filled with self that we habitually think of God in relationship to ourselves, our needs, our desires. But all religion is founded upon what God is and ever was and ever would be had he never uttered the *fiat* of creation."[1] Once we begin to glimpse that truth, our whole approach to prayer (our own and our children's) is immeasurably deepened and illuminated.

As we recognise that prayer is the only means by which our lives may become "worship" in the sense in which we have defined it, many of us will realize at once the sad in-

[1] Bede Frost, *The Art of Mental Prayer*.

adequacy of our very conception of what the practice of prayer involves. For so many people (even instructed Christians) prayer is little more than asking favours of God, letting our requests be made known unto God (Phil. 4.6). The phrase "answers to prayer" has tended to encourage this partial idea. Petitionary prayer is indeed a part, but only a part (and that not the most important) of this total response to God; and even then only in so far as its purpose is to help me, and others, to love and serve God more truly. The final goal of all prayer is that unhindered union (comm-union) of the soul with God to which the union of two personalities in the earthly experience of friendship is the nearest parallel we know. It will include the same ingredients of gratitude, reconciliation (through apology and forgiveness), and request; but those things will not be sought as ends in themselves, but only as necessary expressions of an active friendship which contains them. Once a friendship is established, those other activities arise spontaneously within it; without the friendship they are cold and meaningless. This may explain why for many people the practice of prayer remains only a frigid and barren duty.

The Prayer State Ɛ.

The purpose of all set "times of prayer" and all spiritual exercises (with children as with others) is to cultivate that uninterrupted condition of loving intercourse with God and attention to him which I can only call "The Prayer State"; a state of continuous awareness of God's presence in which /. everything is spontaneously referred to God and kept within the stream of his will and enabling power. This is surely what St Paul meant when he said "Pray without ceasing" , Thess 5:17 (1 Thess. 5.17). That obviously does not mean being consciously aware of God all the time. That would be impossible; because our minds are incapable of concentrating on more than a very limited field of awareness at any moment and a man who is absorbed (as he ought to be) in the immediate demands of his work, or any other legitimate activity, cannot at the same time be engaged in a rapt contemplation of God! Here again the most helpful analogy is that of the lover. A lover is not concentrating his whole attention all the time on the loved one, otherwise his work would suffer (as indeed it sometimes does!); but he is aware all the time of a ground of happiness and wellbeing which colours his whole existence, in which everything is rooted, so that when, at intervals, his mind is not otherwise occupied, he can dwell for a few moments deliberately on his love. Meanwhile all his other activities are being shaped and conditioned, for the most part subconsciously, by the one overriding passion. It is the purpose of prayer to help us to attain that kind of response to God, so that every moment is saturated with a subconscious awareness of him, and the first thought that comes into our minds when we are not otherwise occupied is a thought of him and an opportunity for spending a few refreshing moments deliberately in his presence. That constant, Godward direction of our whole spirit is what we mean by "Adoration" (what I have called the Prayer State), and we see again how it is an attitude of "worship" which embraces every practical item of daily life.

4

Prayer in Practice

WE have spent some time in analysing the theological bases
of prayer because nothing can throw a more penetrating
light on the practice of it, even in its most elementary
forms. It will now be a more simple matter to appreciate
the various kinds of activity which make up the art of
prayer; and at the outset we must recognize that prayer is
indeed an art and must be practised according to certain
recognized "rules". These rules need to be studied and
understood by those who wish to progress in prayer and
to lead others in the way, including the tiniest children.

Three Stages of Prayer *A*.

Before we look together at prayer as an art, it is best to be
clear that there are in fact different degrees, or stages, of
prayer, suited to differing types of spiritual temperament.
It will be useful to isolate three of these. The first is called
Vocal Prayer—speaking to God in "words". This is the *1.*
commonest form of prayer, and it may find expression
either in written prayers (as in the liturgy, as well as in the
scores of little booklets of private devotion of varying
quality) or in our own spontaneous words (extempore
prayer). The second is called *Mental Prayer*, the prayer of *2.*
the mind. This is the kind of prayer that derives its power
from thinking vividly and pictorially about God (chiefly as
he is revealed in the person of our Lord in the narrative
pages of the Gospel) and, without necessarily using any
express words at all, lets the mind be drawn more and more
towards God and thereby allows the whole personality—

thought, feeling, and will—to become saturated with a realization of God's nature and purpose. It is sometimes called "Meditation"—and is really a <u>deliberate activity of thinking about God</u>, <u>in God's Presence, with God's help.</u> It is this Godward inflection which distinguishes it from other kinds of thought; though it is clear that, for a Christian, *all* thinking (even that involved in reading a newspaper or browsing through an illustrated magazine) should be of the nature of meditation. The third kind of prayer we may call generally *Contemplative Prayer*—that <u>inner concentration of the attention on God, without the aid either of words or of deliberate thoughts, which for most people can come</u> (if it comes at all) <u>only as the fruit of a prolonged practice of prayer;</u> though for others (including children) who possess a natural aptitude for it, it may be the most spontaneous expression of their love for God.

It is worth saying here (though we shall remind ourselves of it again later) that <u>a contemplative approach to God often comes more easily to children</u> (with their simple and ready trust) <u>than to more sophisticated adults</u>; and we must be on our guard against allowing a child's prayer life to be too much hampered by the kind of "simple" limits we often set on it. By "simple" we too often mean "easily intelligible", and we may do untold harm to a child's unfolding spirit by trying to compress the great truths and experiences of religion within the narrow compass of his supposed "understanding". The word "simple" really means something much nearer to its German counterpart, *einfach*— "uncomplicated", "single-minded", the kind of attitude Jesus expressed in the phrase "pure in heart", and which prompted that profound saying "Except ye become as little children ye shall not enter into the Kingdom of Heaven" (Matt. 18.3).

These three chief forms of prayer—Vocal, Mental, and

46

Contemplative—must not be regarded as three ascending rungs on a ladder. It is common for writers on the devotional life to speak about "lower" and "higher" levels of prayer and to give the impression that advancing in prayer must involve a series of upward steps from Vocal Prayer through Meditation to some form of Contemplation. Such a view would regard Vocal Prayer as rudimentary, Mental Prayer as more advanced, and Contemplative Prayer as the summit. In practice this idea seems to me erroneous. What distinguishes an advanced state of prayer from a rudimentary one is not the particular form it takes, but the degree of holiness and loving submission to God that it produces in the soul. Some of the most saintly and devoted Christians have never passed beyond the stage of simple vocal prayer; on the other hand, a soul with a natural gift of contemplation may nevertheless fail to exhibit the full fruits of a dedicated life. The response to God is all. Which of these particular expressions of prayer will prove most suitable for any particular soul will depend upon his individual gifts and aptitudes, as well as his varying circumstances; and most people who set themselves to learn and practise prayer as an art will find that they tend to range over the whole field according to the mood and conditions of the moment. Even a natural contemplative, for example, may find at times of great stress or pain that vocal prayer is his only recourse (this was a very common experience during the hazards of the blitz and the other horrors of war); whereas a soul steeped in simple vocal prayer or accustomed to meditation may find itself visited from time to time by a moment of acute awareness and warm response which will induce it to lay everything else aside and simply dwell passively for a while in God's presence. The Curé of Ars tells the story of an old peasant who spent hours on his knees before the Blessed Sacrament, and when the Curé asked him what he said to our Lord in his times of prayer, the old man replied:

47

"I don't say anything. I just look at him and he just looks at me." That is contemplation—an attitude of sustained love and regard which often comes more readily to simple people and to children than it does to more complex minds; but my point is that it may derive from prayer at any of its so-called "levels". In the last resort prayer is always loving attention to God.

Having said all this, it is important to offer the warning that we must be careful—with children as with grown-up people—not to make the mistake of keeping them trammelled by one set practice of prayer which may be unsuited to their particular gifts and which may impede their progress in the spiritual life. Any director must be aware of this danger. Many a person who would find great benefit by learning to meditate has been kept in leading-strings because no one has ever opened up to him the great ranges of prayer beyond the purely vocal; others may go on practising meditation for years, without much profit or consolation, because they long without knowing it for a more spontaneous expression of their love. Both vocal and mental prayer are only means to an end—and that end is a loving response to God expressed through every aspect of life. We must never confuse the means with the end. Get a clear grasp of this, and it will not only assist our own efforts to advance in holiness, but it will also give us sympathy and understanding as we try to teach our children the way of prayer. Remember that quite tiny children, as soon as they get to the stage of enjoying picture-books and asking their profound questions, are already capable of meditation, and even of contemplation, of a much deeper kind than we sometimes realize. The ceaselessly enquiring mind and the "long, long thoughts of childhood" bring them very near to the heart of God. We shall find this thought of enormous importance when we come to consider later some of the problems of children's prayers.

The Art of Prayer B.

We must go on from here to discuss some of the principles and precepts of prayer considered as an art. It is a common saying (with speakers at Missionary meetings, for example): "Even if you cannot *give*, at least you can all *pray*." The reverse is nearly always the truth. Everybody can afford at least sixpence, but very few indeed can offer prayer of any vital power. Any parish priest (and particularly one who hears confessions) realizes that this is so; and it is a <u>terrible indictment of our pastoral system that</u>, <u>speaking generally, we leave our people so poorly instructed</u> <u>—and sometimes not instructed at all—in the ways of</u> <u>prayer.</u> It is all too easy to assume that prayer comes by nature and that people of goodwill and Christian concern can do it without any guidance from their spiritual pastors. This is a grievous error, as my quotation from Bede Frost (p. 36) has emphasized. "To pray, and to teach souls to pray—it is all. For given this, everything else will follow."

Because <u>prayer is an art we need,</u> as with all other arts, <u>to master the principles of it, principles which have been</u> <u>carefully devised and formulated by the great masters of</u> <u>prayer in all ages; and only when we have mastered them</u> <u>ourselves can we teach them effectively to others.</u> The practice of prayer is based on certain rules, tests, and methods of procedure which we need to learn and make our own in practice. But, though prayer is in that sense an art and requires all the severe discipline and application and observance of principle that every art requires, it is nevertheless an art which is open to all who are prepared to submit themselves to the arduous practice and perseverance it demands. Only those who love God and want to love him better will be prepared to accept these disciplines; but the difference between this and other arts is that we all possess in some degree the requisite faculties. What we so often lack is a knowledge of method. How are we to set about it?

C. *Methods of Prayer*

Here I think our best course will be to consider briefly and practically the various stages of a method of meditation taught by one of the greatest of the masters of prayer, St François de Sales, in his classic of spiritual devotion *The Devout Life* (*La Vie dévote*). I choose this for two reasons; first, because it is the simplest and most attractive summary of an approach to prayer which, with minor differences of emphasis, all the great spiritual masters teach in common; and secondly because it is intended for busy people living "in the world" and not for those who possess, in monasteries and convents, a certain spiritual leisure. It is in the teaching of St François de Sales that (in the words of Bede Frost) "the practice of Mental Prayer passes from the cloister into the world". He brings the treasures of mental prayer within the grasp of the ordinary man and woman, and his own divine simplicity and single-mindedness is reflected on every page. It is just this tonic of simplicity (in the true sense of the word) that we most need to brace us, as we learn to pray, against the growing complexities of our age.

All methods of mental prayer, in varying degrees of elaboration, follow the same general plan. They begin with *Meditation*, whereby we focus our thoughts upon God; they pass on to acts of *Affection*, whereby we express to God, through the emotion of love, our admiration, awe, and submission; and they pass into the active affairs of life by means of *Resolution*.

The following table may help us to see how this kind of prayer, deliberately exercised, provides for a complete response of my whole personality to the whole of God (the ultimate "Reality") revealed through the three categories of Truth, Beauty, and Goodness. As we have thought, the total response of the soul to God in prayer is perfectly expressed in the <u>Prayer of St Richard of Chichester, "to <u>know</u> thee more clearly, *love* thee more dearly, and *follow* thee more nearly"</u>.[1]

Activity of the soul	Aspect of personality	Aspect of reality	Form of prayer
Know	Mind	Truth	Meditation
Love	Emotions	Beauty	Affections
Serve	Will	Goodness	Resolutions

An occasional glance at this summary will help to simplify all that now follows.

<u>In *Meditation* I lay my thoughts open to the guidance and illumination of the Holy Spirit</u>; the direction, so to speak, is from God to me. <u>In the *Affections* I make my response to God's love; the direction is from me to God.</u> <u>In the *Resolutions* I seek to allow God's power to come into the very practical affairs of my life and shape them to his will; the direction is again from God to me, and through us both out into the world at large.</u> This simplification may help our thinking about it and our practice of it, though it is of course true that prayer in all its aspects is the work of the Holy Spirit in us (Rom. 8.26) and whatever response we make to God is in itself God's activity. But we see from this simple analysis that prayer is a kind of interplay between my soul and God which has its impact on the world wherever God and I (if I may put it so) touch it together.

The Salesian Method D.

The Method of St François de Sales (sometimes called

[1] Cf. also the famous Prayer of St Augustine of Hippo: "O Thou, who art the light of the minds that *know* thee, the life of the souls that *love* thee, the strength of the wills that *serve* thee: help us so to *know* thee that we may truly *love* thee; so to love thee that we may fully *serve* thee, whom to serve is perfect freedom...".

the *Salesian Method*) follows this general course. I commend it to your further study.

You begin with a definite period of time before you—ten minutes, a quarter of an hour, half an hour, whatever you can honestly manage. Regard that time as sacrosanct and let nothing else, as far as possible, encroach upon it. This in itself is an exacting discipline; but no progress in prayer is possible without such a positive dedication of set times.

(1) *Act of the Presence of God*. Adopt whatever bodily position best disposes your mind to quietness, with perfect freedom to change your position (sitting, kneeling, standing, or walking about) whenever you wish. Then begin with a deliberate act of holding your mind still as you try to realize the Presence of God. This, as we have seen, is a most important preliminary of all prayer, specially in our age of constant distraction. Do not be hurried or anxious about it. Make a quiet place in your mind where you can focus your thoughts on God in complete silence. When your whole being (body and mind) is still and relaxed, let it become occupied with a deliberate remembrance and recollection of God's presence with you. St François de Sales gives four attractive ways of remembering the presence of God, of which the simplest is imagining our Lord himself standing by your side. This is a most important beginning. To embark upon prayer without first realizing the divine presence is like talking into a telephone without being sure that there is anyone at the other end of the line!

(2) *Meditation*. The next step is an Act of Meditation. This may consist of two simple and obvious steps. (i) *The Interior Picture.* You take some short narrative from the Gospel and present it to your imagination in such a way that it lives again in your mind. Picture the event as happening just where you are, within a few feet of where you are kneeling. You may find it helpful (as St Ignatius

Loyola suggests in one of his "methods") to apply your five senses to the scene—to see, to hear, to touch, to taste, to smell. By this simple means you can break down the deadly barriers of familiarity which so often prevent us from penetrating to the heart of the Gospel narrative. For this purpose you may be greatly assisted by reading the Bible in a modern translation, such as the one by J. B. Phillips or the Revised Standard Version. (ii) *The Considerations*. This stage is essential to all meditation. Whether it be a story previously "pictured", or whether it be a passage from one of the Epistles of St Paul (to which the Interior Picture cannot be easily applied) you will now proceed to think it out and ponder on it from every angle that occurs to you. Who said these words? To whom were they spoken? Why did he say them? What does this show me about God and his will? How do I compare with this? How does this affect my life? What ought I to do about this? By such considerations as this God can lead our thoughts to a deeper knowledge of himself; our understanding grows, our love is inflamed, and a passionate desire to serve God can be stimulated in us. "Believe me", says St François de Sales, "there is no way to God save through this door."

(3) *Affections*. Such thoughts, inspired by God, lead naturally to a deepened response of the emotions. All thought (and in fact all activity of any kind) has its accompaniment of emotional response. By deliberately laying our thoughts open to God's influence and by apprehending him more clearly, we find ourselves driven to bow humbly before him "lost in wonder, love, and praise". This affective response involves not only a heightened awareness of God's goodness, love, justice, and power, but also a deeper knowledge of our own evil, selfishness, weakness, and lack of love. In God's presence we begin to see ourselves as God sees us, that is, as we truly are. We find ourselves "judged"

as we measure ourselves thus against God's absolute perfection, and we find ourselves echoing the words of Iago (in *Othello*) when he says of Cassio, "There is a daily beauty in his life which makes me ugly." Thus, in the experience of prayer, the Christian finds that an increasing esteem for God goes hand in hand with a decreasing regard for himself; so that his feelings of love, adoration, and awe are inevitably shot through with feelings of penitence and self-abasement (cf. Isa. 6). All that is included in the emotional response to God which finds expression in the "Affections", and the expression may take the form of spoken words of adoration and penitence, or it may remain unexpressed in the realm of the emotions. However it happens, it is equally an act of love.

4.

(4) *Resolutions*. But such an activity might be nothing more than a kind of spiritual recreation and indulgence unless it is allowed to find an outlet in action, through the will. Emotions indulged for their own sakes are purely sentimental. (That is in fact what "sentimentality" is.) The next step is therefore a deliberate act of the will. "Lord, what wilt thou have me to *do*?" "In what ways", I ask, "can I let this vision of God's love and perfection bear fruit in me?" I then proceed to offer God (with God's guidance) a resolution, a promise of positive and immediate action in some detail of my daily life. It need not be some great and startling reformation. It may be no more than a decision to apologize to someone I have wronged, to pay some outstanding debt, to write some long-delayed letter, to try harder to be patient with some exasperating colleague. But whatever it is, let it be *particular* and *immediate* (not general and remote). By *particular*, I mean some positive and definite matter—"I will pay that particular debt this morning" rather than "I will always pay my debts promptly in future"! And by *immediate* I mean something that can be done straight away rather than something postponed to

an indefinite future—"I will go and apologize to so-and-so tonight" rather than "I will apologize next time I see him." Resolutions often fail because they are too big or too vague and general. "I will always get up when the alarm goes off" or "I will never get angry again" are hopeless resolves. We can only take life step by step as it comes, and victory in a series of minor skirmishes is the surest way to ultimate conquest on the whole front. This is a very practical matter and is in fact the point where religion can and should become healthily uncomfortable. But it is only through such daily resolves (sometimes the rather monotonous repetition of the same one) that I can hope to keep my life at every step in line with God's will for me and come little by little to enthrone God at the heart of all my thoughts and daily activities. The Kingship of God will be slowly set up in me and my whole outlook gradually brought under his dominion; and the results (by continued and renewed resolution) will become more and more apparent in my personal life (home, work, recreations, and friendships) as well as in my social life, my political opinions, and the exercise of my citizenship. My life will begin to become "worship".

This has been no more than the merest sketch, and the reader cannot do better than study it fully in the seven short chapters of the "Devout Life" which contain the Salesian method.[1] My aim has been to illustrate briefly the general purpose and plan of Mental Prayer, because when we come later on to consider the child's approach to the spiritual life we shall see that simple prayer in this form is quite within his compass; and in fact it is only through this kind of prayer that God can ever be established on the throne of our whole life.

[1] Part II, chapters 1–7.

ℰ. *Acts of Prayer*

But, you may well be asking, where do those other activities which we generally comprehend under the term "prayer"—Adoration,[1] Confession,[2] Thanksgiving,[3] Supplication[4]—fit into this scheme? The answer is that within such a growing friendship with God these so-called "acts" of prayer take place spontaneously, almost involuntarily. They are in fact bound to be more or less empty and meaningless, or at the best formal and cold, until we have begun in some small degree to know God and to respond to him in love. Once God is real to us and we begin, as it were, to grow more and more towards him, then all those other kinds of prayer (asking forgiveness, expressing gratitude, making requests for others or ourselves) take on a fresh meaning. They become the normal thing, just as they do in the setting of any friendship; indeed they become so completely natural that you don't even have to make a continual effort to remember them. They just happen. That is why I have felt it worthwhile to spend so much time considering this one important thing that lies at the heart of all the others.

There then is the intimate and personal side of worship, and, even if I have only succeeded in showing something of the depth and range of the prayer life, I hope it may at least help us to approach our children, as they make their first steps, with greater sympathy and humility. Much that I shall want to say later about apparently elementary practical problems of children's prayer and worship will be the clearer for what we have tried to see and understand here.

Summary

Before we proceed now to more objective considerations, let me draw the threads together. We have seen worship as the "all-pervading recognition of the absolute worth of God", embracing both the Ethic and the Cultus and deeply embedded in the Faith. We have seen the Cultus as both social and individual, corporate and personal: the worship of the Christian community and the prayer of the single soul alone with God. We have seen too (one of the many paradoxes of Christianity) that the God before whom we bow in numinous awe is one to whom we can also speak with simple familiarity and tender affection as "Our Father"; and those two strains of Awe and Intimacy are held together in tension in all Christian Prayer and Worship. Children often find this more easy to understand than adults do.

Now that we have gone fairly fully into the underlying truths of worship we may feel ourselves better equipped to deal with some of the many problems of introducing our children to this rich treasure-house of Christian devotion.

5

Training Children in Prayer

A SMALL boy of nine was polishing his boots in the scullery after breakfast one Sunday morning, getting ready to go off to church. His father, settling back comfortably in his armchair by the kitchen fire and opening his Sunday newspaper, called out: "Look sharp there, Tom, or you're going to be late for church", and the boy, with a boot in one hand and the blacking-brush in the other, poked his head round the kitchen door and said: "Dad, when shall I be old enough not to have to go to church any more—like you?"

That kind of situation is repeated in thousands of homes every Sunday. What reply can the father make, in all honesty, to the child's question? There are only two possible answers. One is: "You stick to the Church, my boy. It's the right thing. I ought to be going myself, but I'm just a slacker—so don't take any notice of what *I* do." The other is: "Well, frankly, Tom, I think religion is all right for youngsters like you—I had my share of it when I was your age—but when you get as old and wise as I am ... well, you can drop it." But the important thing to notice is that, whatever the father *says*, it is what he *does* that is going to carry the real weight. The boy is bound to argue, quite naturally, "If my father doesn't think much of all these things the vicar is always talking about, then I suppose there can't be much in them."

a. <u>There are two important facts about children that emerge</u>
l. <u>from that all too common story. The first is that all children</u>
<u>possess a consuming ambition to be grown up.</u> Peter Pan

58

is a sentimental absurdity. Any child in his condition would need psychiatric treatment! The second is that in this desire 2. to be grown up they will always imitate the behaviour of the grown-up people whom they most admire. The whole process of growing to maturity, from infancy onwards, is one of imitation—"As though his whole vocation were endless imitation", as Wordsworth describes it. The ideas and attitudes, the unspoken assumptions as well as the actual behaviour, of grown-up people are all the time influencing children and conditioning them in ways it is impossible to analyse. It is not what I *say*, but what I *am* (the whole complex of temperament, opinions, prejudices, and overt activities constituting my personality) that influence my child in the right or the wrong direction, without a word spoken.

First Impressions B.

This takes us immediately to the heart of all problems connected with the explicit training of children in religion. It is not going to be just a simple question of giving them 1. religious *instruction*—Bible stories, prayers, ethical teaching, and so on (though of course it will involve that incidentally). During those early formative years from infancy N. B. to the age of ten or so, the really vital thing is going to be, not what they learn about religion objectively, but what 2. they come to *feel* about it from their contacts with older people. It is going to be the general impression, pleasant or unpleasant, real or bogus, that will determine whether, in later years, the child will find God or will throw overboard (perhaps scornfully) everything that he imagines religion to be; and the general impression he gets of it will be derived almost entirely from the religious atmosphere of his home, positive or negative. If religion means little or nothing to you, then, however much good sense you may talk, the chances are hundreds to one that your child will be infected by your unspoken attitude. Some wise words are spoken by one of the characters in T. S. Eliot's play, *Family Reunion*: "I think that *the things that are taken for granted at home* make a deeper impression on children than what they are *told*." (Italics mine.) That is the first all-important thing I want to say, and it all boils down to one very challenging fact: If I want my children to love and serve God, then I must first love and serve him myself. That will be the most powerful influence on their whole life. "For their sakes I consecrate myself" (John 17.19).

This is such an important truth that we cannot dwell on it too emphatically; and there is a further aspect of it (concerned with explicit instruction) which we ought to look at before we embark on practical considerations. Archbishop Temple, in one of his early speeches about Christian Education, declared that it is not only useless but positively harmful to appeal to the logical understanding of a child while that understanding is still undeveloped. Instruction must be emotional and imaginative, and given through parable and precept. "The logical element in religion", he said, "must be developed out of the emotional element and not before it, because it would stifle enquiry and paralyse imagination."[1]

That quotation underlines another guiding principle in all that follows. As I have said, the emotional connotation that a child comes to associate with religious experience will depend in the first instance on implicit impressions rather than on explicit teaching; but explicit teaching must be given stage by stage, and such teaching will need to follow this general principle. In the realm of direct instruction, as with the rest of the child's early training in religion, we need to be more concerned about what he feels than about what he knows. If you examine the reasons people

[1] F. A. Iremonger, *William Temple*, p. 92.

give in later life for abandoning the religion of their child-hood, you will find that most of them are simply rational-ized emotions: a deep-rooted distaste provoked by the dull-ness, the boredom, the miserable restraint—sometimes even the thinly disguised humbug—that so often passes for religion. Sometimes, indeed, it may be a radical unwilling-ness to face the moral challenge of Christianity. Most ordi-nary arguments about religion, in pubs and clubs and back-kitchens, are arguments about feelings and personal tastes rather than about theological truth. Very few people aban-don religion on purely intellectual grounds. It is what we *feel*, not what we *know*, which determines what we *do*. G. K. Chesterton once expressed this truth with amusing force in his story of the Professor of Philosophy who spent most of his time proving conclusively that life is not worth living, until one day someone shot a bullet through his tall hat and he ran for his life! We are all far more power-fully actuated by our emotions than by our intellect.

This simple fact (which is not yet clearly enough recog-nized by parents and teachers) bears strongly on the religious training of young children at every point. The most decisive thing we can do, during the first ten years of a child's life, is to put him in the way of gaining a happy and attractive impression of religion, so that he may at least be favourably disposed towards it when the time comes for him to "make up his mind" about it. He will then be in a position to face the intellectual and moral claims of the faith without prejudice; that is, without a distorted emotional attitude. We must try, both by example and by precept, to give him an impression of religion which will appeal to all that is most natural and healthy in him, to his sense of fun as well as to his sense of obligation. It should be "interesting" to the point of fascination. It should be free from all unnecessary restraints and prohibitions, though it must at the same time demand a high degree of

N. B.

discipline (a thing which children both respect and desire). Most important of all, it should appeal at every stage to the child's ambition to be "grown-up"; that is, it should be forward-looking and adult in flavour, avoiding that kind of half-sentimental simplicity which some people think children like, though, in fact, it embarrasses them and confirms them in the idea that religion belongs to childhood and can be abandoned as they grow older.

This kind of religious education begins, for good or ill, with the very earliest impressions a baby receives in his cradle, and it builds up gradually into a "sentiment" (to use a psychological term), which according to its emotional flavour, will one day determine whether the child is going to accept or reject the Christian faith. Because what a young child feels about religion is a more powerful incentive than what he knows about it, we shall, in the earlier stages, regard the imparting of information as only of secondary importance. A child only wants to know more about the things that interest him—and interest (the first business of all educators) is a matter of emotional attraction. If we can help children to associate religious experience with all the things they find most admirable and grown-up and worth taking trouble about, be sure they will ask all the right questions in their own good time and be ready to accept the answers. So much of our direct instruction consists of providing children with ready-made answers to questions they have not yet been prompted to ask. That is a dull and fruitless task, both for teacher and taught. Our aim must rather be to set them in such situations that they ask the right questions with urgent interest. Ninety per cent of sound education is getting people to ask the right questions.

B. *Pre-natal Influence*

How does this work out in practice? Let us look at it from the earliest beginnings. We cannot be certain how soon a child begins to receive impressions. It may be quite soon after he is conceived and certainly some time before he is born. He may be profoundly affected by his mother's state of mind during the period of gestation; so his religious training may well begin as early as that, in the very atmosphere of prayer and dedication with which his mother then surrounds him. Let the child be (so to speak) steeped in an atmosphere of prayer and healthy thinking from the moment of his conception. You may in fact surround him with prayer before he is even conceived and is still only a hope. Prayer is not closely tied to the time-scheme! The mother's thoughts and aspirations will have a quite immeasurable effect on the whole psychic development of the unborn child. Remember Hannah's dedication of the child Samuel before he was even conceived (1 Sam. 1) and Jeremiah's assurance, "Before thou comest forth out of the womb I sanctified thee and ordained thee a prophet unto the nations" (Jer. 1.5). We need to recapture this kind of assurance. There is a whole aspect of ante-natal care which is not taught in the clinics!

C. *Babyhood*

As soon as the child is born his religious education begins in real earnest. At this stage it is impossible to differentiate between religious and any other kind of education—it is *all* religious. The child's first and most formative experience is his relationship with his mother. From this relationship he derives the complex of impressions which will later become his attitude and response to the world at large—and to God. That is an added reason why Mother is such a very important person. To a tiny baby his mother *is* God. She is the source and ground of his existence. She is Providence, supplying all his physical wants and giving him the security, comfort, and encouragement he needs. His whole existence and welfare depend entirely upon her. She is his whole Universe.[1] What mother is and does are giving the child, all unconsciously, his first glimpse of what God is like; those early impressions are terrifyingly powerful and deep-seated and may in fact be indelible. The more we understand about juvenile delinquency, for example, the more we see it as a form of "rejection" which derives in most instances from an unstable and insecure home background, and chiefly from an unhappy relationship with the mother. It is, in a sense, the total rejection of the universe at large, and therefore of God. This underlines most powerfully the point I am making here. The Mother and Child relationship is a profoundly sacred one for more than merely sentimental or emotional reasons. It mediates God to the child.

This is the first step in religious training—and to be aware of this will strongly influence our whole attitude to tiny babies. It is foolish and dangerous to imagine that babies are unimpressionable because they make no obvious response. They are intensely sensitive to atmosphere and may be badly affected by quarrelling or even by any kind of loose or ungenerous talk in their presence. It is always unwise to "talk" in front of young children, even tiny babies. In the same way we should avoid any undue roughness or impatience in our ordinary handling of them. Our whole relationship must be imbued with gentleness and firmness combined; for firmness is a part of true love, though it need never be ungentle. Above all, let the whole relationship be, as far as possible, completely balanced. A child's first need is for a sense of security, and this may be seriously disturbed by that kind of erratic treatment which submits him at one moment to harsh correction and at the next to emotional coddling. Whatever discipline we need

[1] It is this profound truth that is so movingly expressed in the Madonna and Child of Mr Henry Moore in St Matthew's church, Northampton.

to exert should always be evident to the child as part of our love for him—not something that temporarily suspends our love. It is a terrible thing to say to a young child, "If you do that, Mummy won't love you any more"; still more damaging to say, "If you do that, *God* won't love you any more." Remind yourself constantly, "I am all the time introducing this child to God." It is a chastening thought.

But even in the best-regulated households there will be times when mother will lose her temper or give way to nervous irritation. We need not be unduly troubled about such occasions as long as the general setting is one of love and real concern. Children are astonishingly hardy—and very ready to forgive. But it is worth saying here that if ever we do find ourselves betrayed into harsh or unjust treatment, it is a right thing to do with young children what we should do in similar cases with adults—acknowledge our fault quite frankly and forthrightly and make deliberate amends for it; though we shall avoid embarrassing them by being emotional about it. Children have every right to that kind of respect for their personalities, and do in turn respect it. It is a sustained attitude of love and concern which is the all-important thing.

D. Early Prayer Life

After these more general reflections on underlying principles, we can now go on to consider certain more detailed aspects of the child's introduction to religion. His training in prayer can begin as soon as he is born and in his cradle, long before he shows any apparent awareness. Remembering what we said earlier about the child's innate desire to be grown up and his tendency therefore to learn by imitation, our aim from the beginning must be to help him to experience prayer as a natural and interesting thing which grown-up people do as a matter of course. So there is no need to wait until he is old enough to talk. His first direct awareness of prayer should be of praying people. It can be deliberately provided by the familiar sight of father and mother (and perhaps older children) kneeling by his cot, with hands together and eyes closed, praying aloud. Let these external acts of prayer be quite openly demonstrated, but be careful too that it is always a fully reverent act, quiet and composed. In fact, you can say your own prayers and ignore the baby completely. Such a simple prayer-time (which in many homes might become the focus of a revival of family prayer) could consist of a very short act of recollection in silence, an evening collect, the Lord's Prayer said together, perhaps one verse of a simple hymn (not necessarily a children's hymn), and a blessing. For the blessing you may lay your hand lightly on the child's head, so that he becomes familiar with the experience of a sacramental act. In this way the baby is allowed from the very beginning of life to enter into an overt experience of religion—to see and share in a devotional act. Never mind how much or how little he understands of it. He drinks in the atmosphere of it long before he can ask questions about it. He gets a happy impression of people he loves speaking together to Someone present but unseen whom they trust and revere, and he also gets the impression of prayer as something which grown-up people do naturally and regularly. Remember, a child is capable of religious feeling before he is capable of religious thought. So he will grow naturally into accepting the idea of prayer as a normal, adult activity, and as he gets older he will never be able to remember a time when he was not conscious of this attitude to prayer.

Prayer in Infancy

Then in time the inevitable thing will happen, as a matter of course and not of compulsion. In his own time and in his own way the child will begin to take part in these prayer-times—perhaps by putting his hands together and shutting one eye, or perhaps by vocal efforts of various kinds! Don't be too eager to direct these. Let him find his own level at his own pace. In the earlier stages you can still very largely ignore him, so that he feels that he is joining in of his own accord with something which is still primarily *your* activity and not something being foisted on him. You can then begin to lead him along the path of prayer because he wants it himself. He begins to pray spontaneously. You don't just impose it on him. The urge comes from him. "*See - ask - do*"—that is always the order in which young children learn. Far too often it begins with a peremptory "do", and that can have disastrous results.

As he now joins in more and more fully, let prayer times always continue as a common activity—praying together. Avoid any attitude or posture that places the child in a subordinate position and stresses his immaturity. Let him feel all the time that he is being privileged to take his part with you in a grown-up thing. As he gets older, always kneel down side by side with him, as you pray together. In the film *The Rocking Horse Winner* there was a scene in which the mother (who showed no other symptoms of religious concern) gathered her three-year-old daughter, and two older children, to her knees and said "Prayers! Come on now—concentrate!" I thought that perhaps that scene was meant to be funny, but the audience took it quite seriously, and were if anything deeply impressed! Yet that seems to me an almost perfect picture of How Not to Do It. "Prayer at Mother's knee" still has sentimental associations for many people, but there is very little to be said in favour of it. It isolates the child from grown-up people and accentuates his childish subservience, giving him the unspoken impression that prayers are only for children. (After all, he never sees Mummy saying her prayers at Grannie's knee!) It may also obscure the fact that his prayers are addressed to

God and not to his mother—and this may be even more disastrous if any stray aunt or uncle who happens to be staying for the weekend is casually invited to "hear Johnny say his prayers". The worst thing of all is to allow a child's prayer-time to degenerate into an amusing spectacle for visitors. That will certainly be damaging, both to the child and to his religion, a sure way of impressing upon him that prayers are a childish affair. The obvious thing is for father and mother (as well as any older children or visitors who may be allowed the *privilege* of taking part, as long as they know how to behave) to kneel down together, so that they all assume the same status, so to speak, in the presence of the unseen Father of all. Then, by that very act, far more than by anything that is said, the child will come to recognize prayer as a perfectly normal part of everyday activity, as normal as baths and meals and play-times, and, above all, as something which grown-up people value.

This last point is quite crucial, because any child who is allowed to get the impression that "saying your prayers" is an activity peculiar to childhood (like having your nose blown for you or going to bed early) will grow up with a powerful unconscious urge to abandon it as soon as possible. But if he grows into the practice of prayer by slowly aligning himself with what mother and father have always done by his cot, then he will never be conscious of the least compulsion, only of following freely where they lead.

F. *Prayers in Childhood*

What is the next step? Nobody can dogmatize about this, because young children differ so much in their rate and manner of progress, but there are certain broad principles which are useful guides. While the child is still an infant, prayer-time may be no more than mother (and other members of the family when it is possible) saying one or two simple prayers aloud, with hands together and eyes closed.

But when he reaches the toddler stage and begins to be interested in picture books, you may introduce him gradually to the practice of simple meditation by basing your prayer-time on a good picture-book of the life of our Lord.

G. *Picture-books*

Go to some trouble in choosing a good picture-book, because a child's whole outlook on religion is bound to be conditioned by the quality of the experiences it affords. Many a Christian home will boast expensive and elaborate volumes of fairy-tales, with admirable pictures, while the books which are the instruments of religious teaching are often dull, shoddy, and lacking aesthetic merit. That in itself constitutes religious education of a most damaging kind. The contrast is not lost on the small child. He will conclude, with perfect naturalness and impeccable logic, that religion is second-rate. Another important thing to ensure is the inherent *truth* of the pictures we allow children to look at. Be conscious that the pictures that we (sometimes so casually) allow children to see are shaping their whole conception of God and the world. Many religious pictures are not only cheap and shoddy as works of art, but are also (what is much worse) superficial and sentimental in their presentation of fact.

H. *Presenting the Character of Christ*

The most obvious instance of this is the feeble presentation of the person of our Lord so much favoured by second-rate religious artists, portraying him as an effeminate and rather pathetic figure that can make very little appeal to healthy-minded children. In a few years' time, characters like Dan Dare will be their heroes, and we must show children a Christ who possesses (as indeed he does) all the heroic virtues of Dan Dare and a great deal more besides. It is not really surprising that the emasculated Christ we so often offer to children is soon overshadowed by lesser heroes. I make no apology for stressing this with all the emphasis I can. We must present our Lord, in both picture and story, as possessing all the virile and adventurous qualities which children rightly admire; and this will have a strong bearing on our choice of suitable picture-books. We may have to exercise a censorship over the poorer kind of literature (often presented in all good faith by well-meaning friends or godparents) and keep them away from our children as we keep away all other harmful influences. Have one really good and carefully chosen book (not many) and let it become the focus of prayers all through childhood. The best book for this purpose is William Hole's *Jesus of Nazareth* (Eyre and Spottiswoode),[1] containing eighty pictures of our Lord's life. The pictures, in water colour, are good as simple works of art; the figure of our Lord is manly and attractive and consistent throughout; the topographical details are accurate. The Gospel story, in the Authorized Version, is printed opposite each picture, and at the end there are scholarly notes that will help parents to build up the details of the pictures imaginatively. This book makes an admirable christening gift and will last a life-time. It can also be given to a child at Confirmation, to a young couple as a wedding present, or to an ordinand at his ordination. It has a universal appeal and is an invaluable aid to prayer and meditation at all stages.

1 Meditation through Pictures

I have spent this time considering the merits of a good book because nothing can be more important as we try to enrich and deepen a child's early experiences of prayer. Such a book can become the secure foundation of a whole lifetime of devotion. If it is quite obviously the best and most attractive picture-book in the house, and if it is always

[1] Recently republished at 30s.

handled with particular care and regarded as a special treat (even though it may be used every day), that in itself will do a great deal to evoke in the child a sense of reverence and respect for religion. As the child sits on your knee and turns over the pages, he is being introduced to the practice of meditation. In the earlier stages this may consist of nothing more than looking at one or two pictures and letting the child ask questions about them. He absorbs, first through the pictures alone and later by question and narrative, an impression of our Lord which will command first his liking, and later his affection and worship. Your prayer-time, then, may consist of looking together at a few pictures, dealing with questions and comments (which is meditation), and then saying, "Well, Jesus is with us now, so shall we kneel down together and talk to him." By this kind of meditation we can help the child to build up in his mind a strong and attractive picture of our Lord, who will be all the time the focus of interest. We shall watch him healing sick people, helping people who are sad or in trouble, always thinking of others. The child will respond to these vivid pictures of our Lord's goodness, kindness, and strength, and his simple admiration can at a very early age develop into a deep affection.

I suggest that, for the purpose of prayer, it is always wiser to focus all attention on our Lord as a *man*, or at least as an *older boy*. I would seriously question whether, at this early stage, it is wise to lay too much emphasis on the "Baby Jesus". The stories of the Nativity will be told and re-told with delight, but it is a mistake to encourage a child to offer prayer and worship to the Baby Jesus. Remember that a child of two or three already feels vastly superior to a baby, and we must always appeal to his constant desire to be grown up. Let the children enjoy to the full the stories of our Lord's infancy, but let all their prayer be addressed to Christ in his perfect Manhood.

6

So, as you look together at your picture-book, commenting and questioning, you are praying in a very profound sense. The child very soon grasps the thought that our Lord is ever present and finds no difficulty in talking to him quite naturally about the things that interest him, thanking him for the day's pleasures, asking him to bless friends (especially those who are ill), and commending everyone to his care. You will need to offer a little guidance here, but let the child himself do most of the work.

Free or Formal?

This raises the next question, what sort of material are we to use in our prayers? Is it good to use a book of prayers, or should we always say prayers out of our own heads? Must we be formal or informal? Children are equally at home with either kind of prayer, and within a clear, devotional framework we can be free to ring the changes more or less at will. By all means use formal prayers; and here (as with everything else) always use the best. Don't hesitate to introduce children at a quite early age (any time after three) to some of the greatest prayers and hymns of the Christian tradition. Children are fascinated by the grandeur of fine words and derive from them a deeper experience than we sometimes recognize. My own children from the age of three have loved the Compline prayers, especially "Be present, O merciful God, and protect us through the silent hours of this night . . ." You may ask, what do phrases like "changes and chances of this fleeting world" and "repose upon thy eternal changelessness" mean to a three-year-old? There is no telling. Experience suggests that children absorb as a kind of atmosphere the purport of great Christian affirmations and assurances long before they can be expected to grasp their meaning intellectually.[1]

[1] "People take in, without knowing it, what comes to them as an *atmosphere* . . . they are more easily taught through the heart in its wildness than through the head in its regularity" (Fr Benson).

This is a revealing educational truth. For example, this Compline prayer no doubt conveys the impression of God surrounding them with unchangeable love and care even though life has its disappointments and hard moments: "underneath are the everlasting arms". There is a great saying of T. S. Eliot about Poetry which applies equally to the language of devotion: "True poetry can communicate before it is understood." Be guided by this truth and don't be deterred by the fear that children will not understand. Many of the Prayer Book collects and other traditional prayers are just as intelligible to children (and far more lovely) as some of the "simple" inanities we are often tempted to substitute for them. Books like *My Own Picture Prayer Book* and *My Own Picture Hymn Book* (both published by the S.C.M. Press) are an excellent guide for young children's prayer-times. Formal prayers need great and memorable words. Quite young children enjoy the sonorous phrases of the Lord's Prayer, the Creed, and some of the Psalms and Canticles. The Benedicite, for example, with its echoing refrain "Praise him and magnify him for ever", is a great favourite with children. After all, they will go on repeating these magnificent words to the end of their lives without ever exhausting the treasures of meaning contained in them. It is good to let them have their minds stocked with the great classical prayers and hymns of Christendom, and to begin as early as possible.

For the more simple and intimate part of our prayer-time we may encourage children to talk to our Lord quite spontaneously in their own words, never mind how crude and familiar they may sometimes seem to us. Give them complete freedom and never be shocked by anything they say. To them the whole field of experience is religion (and quite rightly) and they will pass without any difficulty from the measured words of the Benedicite or Psalm 23 to such a homely petition as "Please God, don't let Mummy forget it's my birthday on Tuesday!" The matter of these more informal prayers may well be largely determined by the pictures which have been the subject of our "meditation". For example, if it was the picture of our Lord healing a leper, we could include a simple act of thanksgiving acknowledging our Lord's kindness and care for people: "Thank you, Jesus, for making people better." We could then think briefly of any people we know who are ill (Grannie or Uncle George, or the little boy next door), and ask our Lord to bless them and help them to get well again. We can look back over the day and thank him for the things we have enjoyed—which may include anything from an iced lollie to a new pair of knickers!—and end by commending ourselves to God's care for the night, either informally ("God bless us all and be with us tonight as we sleep") or formally with such words as "Into thy hands, O Lord, I commend my spirit..." or "Lighten our darkness"... There is room for infinite variety and constantly changing interest.

relevant prayers:

κ. *Penitence* ᵛ.⁸

We have not included the element of confession here. How is that to be approached with young children? This is not a matter about which there will be general agreement, but my own inclination is to treat the question of children's "naughtiness" as lightly as possible. We are generally inclined to take it far too seriously. If the child has done anything really naughty during the day, he can quite simply tell God, as well as his mother, that he is sorry about it and ask help to be good. But it is harmful to insist on that unless he really is sorry, and the best plan is to treat it in a positive way—"Please help me to be a good boy, as you want me to be"—rather than to extract expressions of sorrow which may mean very little. A good deal of childish "naughtiness" is due to high spirits, or to self-assertion

74

against some oppressive or unjust situation. An adult can express a feeling of frustration in words or by some form of self-defence. To a young child there may be no recourse except to sulk or pull his baby sister's hair or smash a toy to bits. Again, a good deal of so-called "naughtiness" may be simply part of his constant exploring and experimenting. We need to make a careful distinction between the kind of misbehaviour which is merely inconvenient to adults (such as making a noise or swinging on the curtains or emptying the coal scuttle over the best carpet) and the kind of misbehaviour which derives from original sin, such as lying, stealing, or temper. But even these should not be treated with a too heavy hand. It is far more important to discover why the child is tempted to do these things and then to deal as far as possible with the cause. Lying may be due to fear of punishment, or to vivid imagination; stealing to a feeling of being unduly deprived; temper to a sense of frustration; and it often happens that, with a deeper understanding of the causes of misbehaviour, we can meet the child more than half way. Harsh and censorious correction may drive the trouble deeper, and a sentimental or emotional approach is even more questionable. Let the whole treatment of "sin" be perfectly unemotional and matter-of-fact—no emotional scenes, no playing on the child's immature feelings or sense of honour, no misusing of prayer-time as a means of appealing to his better nature, or bribing him to be good. The best way of all is that, without any explicit pointing of the moral, the child should come to recognize the positive goodness, kindness, gentleness, and strength of our Lord's character during the times of meditation and should learn to measure himself, as he grows older, against that standard. It is impossible to lay down hard and fast rules about this; but these few reflections may be a helpful guide as we try to lead children to an understanding of penitence. In the earlier stages it is best to err on the side of leniency and to overlook as much as possible.

L. *Rebellion!*

The question often arises, "What am I to do if my child flatly refuses to say his prayers one night? Should I compel him? or should I let him go his own way?" This is a quite serious problem if you use the old-fashioned method of prayer "at mother's knee". You obviously cannot compel, because that exaggerates still further the impression that prayers are a thing that children do because grown-ups tell them to! And if you let him go his own way, there is no telling where the rebellion will stop. This problem illustrates the immense importance of all I have tried to say about "praying together". If the child is in the habit of saying his prayers with you, kneeling side by side, the difficulty is less likely to arise; and if it does the solution is a simple one. You can reply, without being the least bit hurt or anxious: "All right, you carry on with what you're doing, if you want to . . . but I'm going to say my prayers as usual." Then you can kneel down and say your own prayers, leaving the child to his own devices. But be careful to do it without any hint of irritation or disappointment and, of course, avoid being smug about it. Never let any element of strain or compulsion enter into prayer-times. A child is so eager to conform to grown-up custom that he will not remain a rebel for long. The chances are that he will be kneeling at your side before you have finished. But never mind if he holds out for one night. At any rate you have done nothing to drive the resistance deeper; and if, on the following night, you simply carry on as usual without further comment, you will probably find that the whole thing has been completely forgotten.

M. *A Prayer Corner*

A picturesque way of turning prayer-time into a very

special occasion is <u>to have a Prayer Corner.</u> It need not be
a very elaborate affair and the idea can be adapted in dozens
of different ways. A corner of the bedroom or living-room
can be set apart as a special place for prayers. You may have
a small table or prayer desk, with a cross or crucifix or a
favourite picture. If you can't have a special table you can
always use the corner of a dressing-table or some other
suitable piece of furniture. <u>Children will take great pleasure
in adorning the prayer corner with flowers and other
decorations.</u> It is a good plan to have two candles on the
table and to have a simple little ceremony of lighting them
as a prelude to prayers. <u>Children love lighting candles,</u> and
candle-light creates a perfect atmosphere for quiet prayer.
Let the child light the candles first and then switch off the
other lights. <u>This has the effect of turning the prayer
corner into a brilliantly lighted focus for worship in the
darkness of the surrounding room, and also of marking off
the time of prayer as a specially</u> dedicated time. The child
can put the lights on again and extinguish the candles when
prayers are over. This not only engages attention and pro-
vokes interest, but it is a most effective way of making a
simple line of demarcation betwen prayer-time and other
time. (Incidentally, this use of candlelight to focus a special
place is most effective if ever you have to conduct evening
prayers for a small group of children—Scouts or a Club—
in an ugly parish hall. Candlelight is a lovely thing in itself,
and by using it like this in a corner you can virtually
obliterate the rest of the hall and make the focus wherever
you want it.)

focus with Candles.

Summary

Our concern so far has been entirely with the child's
training in personal and private prayer, which is where
he is bound to begin. We shall see later that this should not
be separated from his share in the life of the Church, the

divine society of which he is made a member in his baptism; but most of his earlier growth in religion will inevitably be along such lines as we have sketched. It is impossible to devise a completely detailed scheme because no two children are alike, and even within a single family there will have to be infinite variety and adaptation. But these broad principles will give adequate guidance at every stage to discerning and sympathetic parents. All I have tried to say about a child's first approach to religion comes to a focus in that one outstanding principle which I have continually stressed—that we must help our children to grow spontaneously into an experience of prayer as a normal, healthy, adult thing which can command their respect, and appeal at each successive stage to their desire to be grown-up people.

If you will read this chapter over again in conjunction with Chapters 3 and 4 you will see how the approach we have outlined does in fact provide for a very profound experience of prayer in all its forms. *Vocal Prayer* (whether formal or extempore) must obviously loom large; but *Mental Prayer* (Meditation), with all its accompanying "acts", can be gradually induced from simple beginnings in the picture-book, as the child learns to use his imagination on the Gospel story and to think out its meaning for his own life and the life of other people. Within that simple setting we can help him to make his own "acts of prayer"— Adoration, Confession, Thanksgiving, and Supplication— and as he grows older (bearing in mind the precautions we must be sure to take about fostering too early a crippling sense of guilt) we can show him how to make resolutions to overcome, with God's help, the things he will come to recognize as "sinful". But here, as with everything else, he will learn more powerfully by seeing the same thing at work in us; and if you are willing to say "Mummy is sorry she was so cross today; she is going to ask Jesus to help her not to be cross tomorrow" it will earn the child's complete respect and help him to make similar resolves himself with no feeling of undue compulsion. Above all, if you get into the way of using periods of silence as a regular part of prayer-times right from the beginning, you will give the child opportunities of laying his mind open to the influence of the Holy Spirit and allowing God to deal with him at his own level. In this way a child may have experiences of a contemplative kind, deeper and richer than we can tell; at any rate he is learning to put himself into the right condition of mind for God to confront him.

N. *Independence*   μ.ᵐ.

One last thing. When are we to allow him to become completely independent and say his prayers on his own? This is another of those questions which cannot be answered generally. Some children will want to do so round about the age of nine or ten; others will enjoy corporate prayer for much longer. I suggest that it is a wise thing to begin preparing for a child's independence any time after the age of six or seven. Once he has become well set in a habit of prayer of the kind we have described, let there be occasions when you pray together silently. You may say, "Tonight let us say our prayers quietly in our own minds." At the beginning of this new step you may still find it necessary to give some guidance aloud as you proceed through the various stages of prayer-time: "We'll begin by thinking of Jesus with us. . . . Now let's look at our picture and think about it. . . . Shall we thank God now for anything we've enjoyed today? . . . Whom shall we pray for? . . . What do we want Jesus to help us with tomorrow? . . ." and so on. Leave silent pauses at each point and let the child say his own prayers, while you say your own. Later on you may take this a step further by encouraging the child now and again to say his prayers entirely on his own, as you kneel with him and say yours. This will avoid the danger of letting him become too dependent on your guidance and

semi at 6 or 7

guidance

Completely

12 or 13

initiative. Later still it will be possible to give him occasions when he can be entirely independent: "You're getting a big chap now. Would you like to say your own prayers this evening, and I'll say mine later?" But we shall have to be guided entirely by the child's nature and progress; and in a family of several children there will be variations due to differences of age and mutual relationships. But by adopting in general this deliberate policy of encouraging independence we shall be preparing the child for the time when, in the nature of things, he will have to break loose and stand on his own feet. If we can be confident that he has during those earlier years become acquainted with prayer in all those different aspects there will be no need for us to be anxious when he starts off on his own independent devotional life. The more intimately we have shared with him the experiences of prayer the more likely he is to want to keep us in touch with his progress, to ask advice and help, and to share with us the religious concerns of adolescence. If he has grown up to think of prayer as an adult

good!

thing he will naturally want to go on advancing in maturity and will not feel tempted to lay it aside with other "childish things" when he becomes a man.

Note: We have made no attempt to deal here with the two subjects of *Grace before Meals* and *Family Prayers*. We have been concerned only with the basic principles of training in personal prayer. Within that larger setting we shall be wise to cultivate the practice of recollection and thanksgiving at other times of the day, and Grace is one of the most effective means of encouraging this. We have seen too how the practice of prayers round the baby's cot may become the nucleus of a family prayer-time and there can be no more effective way of establishing such a practice. But the details will have to be worked out according to the particular situation and needs of each family.

6

Children's Questions *terminology?*

BEFORE we go on to deal with the other side of a child's approach to religion—the communal worship of the Church —we must look carefully at another big problem which bears closely on his growing understanding of the Faith— a thing of immense importance if the child is to get a happy and right impression from the start—and that is all that comes under the general heading of "children's questions". We know how very baffling some of these can be, and how we often hesitate how to answer them, not only because we may be unsure of the answer ourselves, but also because we wonder how much the child can grasp, or are anxious in case the full answer should disturb or unsettle him. Are there any general principles that can give us practical guidance in answering children's sometimes profound queries? Fortunately there are, but before we look at them it may be helpful to think a little about the nature of their questions and the states of mind they often reveal.

Perhaps I can do this best by one or two personal references which seem to me to typify the problem. One afternoon, when he was six, my eldest boy went with his mother to a young wives' meeting where a visiting speaker was describing the work of one of our most famous orphanages. In the evening I was saying prayers with him at bed-time and he suddenly said, quite out of the blue, "Will they take me away from you and Mummy like that man said?" I had heard nothing about "that man", so I asked what he had been saying, and the child explained: "The man said they took little boys and girls away from their homes and put them into Banana Houses." He was obviously quite troubled about it, and I was frankly puzzled. I had no idea what he imagined Banana Houses to be, but they were clearly frightening him and causing him acute anxiety. I went downstairs and asked my wife what "that man" had been talking about—and then the thing became quite clear. I was able to go upstairs again and assure him that Dr Barnardo's Homes were run by kind people who looked after boys and girls who had lost their parents! He was enormously relieved, and, after we had included in our prayers a special remembrance of orphan children and the people who looked after them, he went off to sleep with a load lifted from his mind. The bogey had been dispelled.

That simple incident illustrates two further facts about the young child which will help us to deal imaginatively with his questions (spoken or unspoken) and sometimes to forestall his fears. One is his constant need for reassurance; and the other is the ease with which he will create quite terrifying, imaginative bogeys out of a simple misunderstanding of words. As we go on thinking about the child's first steps in religion let us look closely at these two things. They go very deep.

A. *The Need for Reassurance*

First, his need for reassurance. As the child grows out of babyhood he begins to realize that the world is not such a comfortable and friendly place as he once thought. He finds it full of hard and hostile forces which are trying to frustrate him. He is no longer the undisputed centre of his secure little universe. Things are against him and he begins to know fear. Sometimes these fears may be caused by things that look trifling to us; sometimes they may be the sort of thing that a child cannot even express to us at all. We need to be very much aware of this, because these early fears and frustrations, specially if they become closely associated in his mind with God and religion, may have a profound effect on his whole personality which later training will not be able to root out. They are often the reason why he breaks away from religion in later life, though the explanation he gives for doing so may not always be (and generally isn't) the real one. That is why we have got to go out of our way to make sure, so far as we can, that fears and misimpressions are removed before they become rooted, and that the child is given a strong sense of security and reassurance. And this will be constantly affecting the way we present religious truths to children and particularly the way we handle their questions and perplexities.

Let me give, as a further illustration of this point, another personal experience with my eldest boy. This again occurred when he was about six. He had grown up to think of God our Father as kind and considerate; and then he suddenly had to face a quite shattering problem when he was badly stung by a wasp. He had always been rather nervous of wasps and now the thing came to a perplexing issue for him: "If God is kind, why did he let that wasp sting me? *quest.* Why did he give wasps stings at all to hurt people with? That's not *kind*!" This was the problem that confronted us at prayer-time, and he was most emphatic about it. It is the perennial problem of the love of God and the suffering of the world. I suggested that perhaps God gave wasps a sting so that they could defend themselves against people who tried to hurt them. I said, "I expect that wasp thought *ans.* you were going to swat him, so he got in first!" This produced a smile. He appreciated the point. "Then there's another thing", I said, "now that you've been stung by a wasp and know it's not as bad as you thought, you won't be so afraid of wasps any more, will you?—and what's more, you'll be able to help other people who are afraid of them." Within the limits of his understanding and experience, I am sure all that was perfectly *true*—and it was certainly reassuring. The problem goes deeper than that, of course, but at any rate he saw that God might allow wasps their stings without being unkind; and <u>he saw too that something good might come even out of the discomfort of a wasp's sting</u>. The upshot was that we included in our prayers that night a Thanksgiving for the wasp's sting! That illustrates what I mean by trying at every point to meet a child's fears and problems by giving him a sense of security in the face of an increasingly hostile world. If he once gets the impression that God is hostile, it will be all up with his religion.

This general principle bears closely on the whole problem of children's questions. They will crop up at any time of the day or night, though prayer-time often gives the best atmosphere for dealing with them, because then, whatever the nature of the question, it can always be given a clearly Godward inflection. It is true that some questions may need an immediate and urgent reply. They can't wait. We must satisfy the enquiring mind while the interest is still warm. But with others, of a more general kind, we may often reply, "Let's leave that question till prayer-time tonight and then we'll think about it together very carefully." This will also give us the opportunity, with very difficult questions, of thinking about them beforehand and preparing our reply in the most effective terms. They become material for Meditation.

B. ### ANSWERING CHILDREN'S QUESTIONS

There are one or two quite simple rules about answering children's questions, whether directly religious or otherwise, and they all derive from these underlying considerations we have just sketched.

1. ### *The Sense of Security*

The first is that all our <u>answers</u> to his questions about God and death and suffering and heaven <u>should be, within</u>

the limits of his understanding, the sort of answers that will satisfy this need for security and not undermine his trust. But this does not, of course, mean that we must be reassuring at all costs, quite regardless of truth. There are some agnostic thinkers who would take the view that the Christian "myth" (even though they do not themselves believe in it) is a useful means of reassuring children while they are young, and that when they get older they can safely discard it, together with their belief in fairies and hobgoblins! This view has been explicitly stated on the radio by one eminent psychiatrist. One could only regard that as a shocking violation of a child's confidence, because as he grows out of infancy into childhood his one urgent concern is always "Is it true?" So truth and reassurance must clearly go together; and we can be profoundly grateful that the truths of the Christian faith—in the face of sin, suffering, and death—are the most reassuring answers in all the world to every conceivable perplexity that life presents. So besides giving the child the kind of answer that will strengthen his confidence in God's love, we must be sure that it is an answer which fully preserves the truth about God.[1] The two aspects are quite inseparable.

2. Questions about Death

Look at one or two examples. *Death* can be a terribly menacing thing to a young child, and the sight of grief and the grim trappings of a funeral may set up in his mind doubts and conflicts about God's love which can cause him acute distress. I once had to deal with a young boy of eight whose whole trust in God was badly shaken by the death of

[1] Dr Iremonger, in his life of Archbishop Temple (p. 172), tells the story of a West Country miner, the leader of a miners' Bible Study Group, who always began by saying, "Whatever we think or say, boys, *let us be sure we keep clear the character of God.*" That is a perfect precept for answering children's questions.

his mother. Some well-meaning relative had remarked in the child's presence that God had "taken her" and another had asked petulantly why good people had to die young when bad people went on flourishing to a ripe old age. It was the kind of talk that so often surrounds a bereavement, and the child's confidence was shattered. He hated God, because he was allowed to believe, without any qualification, that God had "taken her" from him, and he resented it with hot rebellion. But if we are careful right from the very beginning to let children take account of death as something quite natural—passing into a world where everything we most love in this world will be at its best and where God wants us all to be one day—they will readily accept death without fear or resentment. In other words, interpret death to the child in the light of God's love and care for us shown in Jesus Christ, being careful all the time to speak about it in a way that makes God lovable and attractive and good. No doubt there will be many details we shall have to fill in later, but at this stage it is all-important that the truth as we present it should be deliberately reassuring and free from anxiety.

Perhaps we should note, in passing, that children may be confronted with perplexing thoughts about death, suffering, or wrong-doing at a very early age. At the age of five I remember being haunted for days by the sight of a sparrow, which had collided with some telephone wires, writhing on the ground in its death agonies. Children cannot—and ought not to be—protected unduly from the problems of life in the raw; and we need not be anxious about the effect of such experiences if we are ready to give them the Christian Faith in all its fullness. Many people think that a child's religion should be concerned only with "happy things"; but, unless we give him the whole faith that will answer the dark problems as they come, his religion will fail him just at the point where it is intended to meet his need. It is not entirely surprising that so many children later abandon that kind of easy, pleasant religion as something unrelated to real life.

3. The Need for Truth

All our replies, then, besides preserving the integrity of God's love, must be *strictly true*—though obviously within the limits of the child's understanding. We are sometimes tempted to tell half-truths and even fairy-tales to children, because we are afraid that the full truth (about such subjects as death, evil, judgment, heaven, and hell) will shock him. It is right instinct to want to avoid shocking him, but it is most important that we should never for that reason tell him anything that he will have to unlearn later. The very fact that he asks a question at all shows that he is capable of understanding at least part of the answer, and, even if he does not need the whole answer to begin with, whatever part of the answer he is ready for must be in itself substantially true. Knowledge grows like a tree; it is an organic process, and later knowledge must be fully consonant with earlier. The example I gave above about death illustrates how an answer can be both true and reassuring, without going into the *full* truth, which can be safely left until he gets a little older and asks further questions.

Take, for instance, a very common type of question about death. The child's pet dog, Fluffy, has just died and in his grief the child asks: "Shall I have Fluffy again when I go to heaven?"—or, perhaps, more simply, "Has Fluffy gone to be with Jesus?" What is the answer? If you say "No" the child's simple faith in God and heaven is upset. God is unkind—and the child does not want to go to Heaven if Fluffy won't be there. I suggest that the true answer, within the natural limitations of the child's understanding and affections, is "Yes". This answer not only confirms the child in his trust in God's love for Fluffy, and preserves his

idea of Heaven as an attractive place where he wants to be
when the times comes; it is also, I suggest, essentially true.
Whatever else the Beatific Vision may be, we can be sure
that it will include the complete fulfilment and satisfaction of
all our legitimate desires and affections, of which the child's
love for Fluffy is a most important part. Such an affection
is the beginning of altruism and of a very high quality. So
the answer is "Yes"—and later on, when the child is better
equipped to question more deeply, he will be able to weigh
up, without prejudice, the age-long problem of whether
animals have souls and whether we shall actually recover
their companionship in heaven, or not. But as he grows in
his love for God and knowledge of the world he will eventually be able to take those deeper problems in his stride, and
will at any rate be helped to recognize that his early affection for Fluffy must certainly have its counterpart in the
complete fulfilment that Heaven will afford. I have thought
it worth while to deal with that particular question in some
detail, because it so admirably illustrates how the answer to
a rather puzzling question (and one that we might be
inclined to treat flippantly), can at the same time "preserve
the character of God", reassure the child, and be in substance perfectly true to the Christian revelation within the
limits imposed by the child's immature understanding.

My own children, as we have discussed death and the
after-life, have always wanted to know whether there
will be toys in heaven—as well as ice-cream and other
delights. This question presents the same problem in a
lighter vein, but at heart it is equally important. Here again
I am sure that the answer for a four-year-old is "Yes—the
very best toys and the nicest possible ice-cream"; because
it is true that the gratification these things represent for a
young child will have, so to speak, their spiritual counterpart in that supreme satisfaction that the vision of God will
give. The fact that a child interprets happiness in terms of

88

material delights—fun and games and nice things to eat—
is beside the point. If he is to grasp the truth that Heaven
is a happy place and that God fully intends it to be, he can   good!
only be expected to visualize it in his own simple categories
of happiness. We must be careful never to present him with
an idea of Heaven which he would regard as a deprivation
and almost as a punishment. There will be time enough for
him later on to complete the picture with more spiritual
conceptions of happiness when his experience of life provides him with them.

4. *Questions about Evil and Suffering*

Whenever he asks questions about evil and hell, we must,
on the same principle, be careful to ensure that he understands that evil is something that God does not want and
is helping us to overcome, and that hell (whatever else may
be involved) means people deliberately shutting themselves
away from God's love. (It is rather like a child shutting
himself up in a cupboard or running into the garden,
because he is afraid to face Mummy when he knows he has
done something wrong. Children readily appreciate that
illustration.) But it is not God's doing—God loves and
wants everybody.

Again, his questions about illness and suffering will find
ready and reassuring answers as we contemplate together
our Lord's dealings with sick and suffering people. The
picture of our Lord healing the leper or comforting the
widow of Nain is worth far more than any amount of
abstract explanation. The child's question is answered
almost before he asks it—or at least the answer is awaiting
him (in the picture) as soon as he becomes aware of the
problem.

So, at every stage, we shall be conscious of this need to
"stick to the truth" and preserve the child's confidence in
God's complete trustworthiness. At the lowest level we shall

avoid ideas like "If you do that sort of thing, God won't love you", and at a higher level we shall be extremely careful in our handling of Old Testament stories (like the story of Uzzah or the story of Elisha and the bears) where sub-Christian ideas have survived into the Christian tradition. A general reply to a child's perplexities about Old Testament "barbarities" might be: "That is what people in those days used to *think* God was like, but since Jesus came we know that he is not really like that at all, and doesn't want that sort of thing." With very young children the emphasis should always be on the person of our Lord, and any Old Testament stories we see fit to tell them (naturally avoiding the more primitive and bloodthirsty ones) can be told simply as "stories that Jesus learnt when he was a boy". We may sometimes even remind them that Jesus deliberately contradicted crude Old Testament ideas (Matt. 5 *passim*)[1] and that *he* is the one we depend on for the full truth about God's love and care for us.

5. *Questions about Sex*

One outstanding and crucial instance of where we must never be tempted to depart from the substantial truth is the answer we give to questions about sex (which incidentally determine more powerfully than we sometimes recognize a child's whole response to "authority"). When a child first enquires where he came from he is asking a most urgent question which goes, in a sense, to the roots of all being. It is nothing short of criminal to fob him off with fairy-tales about storks or gooseberry bushes or doctors' bags. Such stories can give him no particular reverence for his origin; and later, when he discovers that you have deceived him over such an important matter, he will not only be inclined to despise your authority, he may even be

[1] "Ye have heard that it was said by them of old time . . . but *I* say unto you . . .".

inclined to mistrust all authority of any kind. I think this goes very deep indeed. Even the tiniest child, old enough to formulate this question, is capable of accepting the answer that <u>he grew out of his mother's body in much the same way as fruit grows on a tree</u>. (By all means use "gooseberry bushes" if you like, but use them sensibly!) He doesn't need the whole answer to begin with. That fact will be quite exciting enough to satisfy him—and it is, after all, far more remarkable and estimable than any nonsense about storks and gooseberry bushes. It will give him an immense respect and regard for his mother, as well as for himself; and we shall of course emphasize the truth that this is God's own miraculous method of creating new life. Later on, when he wants to know more about how this wonderful process started, see that he gets the answer he wants. If he does not get it from you, he will get it from much less desirable sources, and <u>it is wise to remember that a child may be quite capable of grasping the remarkable processes of reproduction any time after the age of six or seven.</u> People often hesitate to answer these questions frankly, partly because they themselves feel embarrassed, and partly from a mistaken idea that the knowledge will somehow disturb and shock children. There is nothing the least bit disturbing about such knowledge and a child who acquires it cleanly and explicitly from the ones he loves most, and who were the agents in his own procreation, will find it much easier as he grows older to resist unworthy ideas and attitudes. Incidentally, always use recognized technical terms (instead of childish euphemisms) for the various parts of the body.[1] They are just as intelligible and easy to say

[1] Books on Reproduction for children, published by the S.C.M. Press: *Puzzled Parents* (answering children's question), 1s.; *Where Did I Come From?* (for young children), 6d.; *How a Family Begins* (for girls), 9d.; *The Start of a Family* (for boys), 9d.; *Science and You* (a more detailed account of reproduction), 1s. These are all admirable books for parents and children.

as the "baby" words we sometimes think more appropriate, and they have an adult flavour that commands his respect. This is a perfectly clear instance of where later knowledge needs to grow organically out of earlier knowledge and where every stage must be substantially the truth.

Finding out Together

Another simple rule about answering children's questions is: If you don't know the answer, say so. Children do not in fact expect us to be unfailing oracles (that is a myth we like to build up for ourselves!). They will not think any the less of you for being honest; and will respect frank ignorance much more than pretended knowledge that later proves false. With the best will in the world, we are continually being caught out by our children's incisive questioning, and in that case the best reply is "I am afraid I don't know the answer to that one—let's go and find out together." A piece of common research is an unfailing delight to any child who is really eager to know. It is pretence and falsity that shatter his confidence. But there is no need to be caught out too easily if we are careful to prepare ourselves beforehand for the kind of questions that we know children will inevitably ask. Questions about their origin, for example, are certain to come sooner or later. No parent ought ever to be taken off his guard with that one! The same is true of questions like "Who made God?" Be ready for them. We need not only the knowledge, but the terminology for expressing it; and all that is readily available if we will take as much trouble to prepare for our children's questions as some people do to fill in their football coupons or their income tax returns.

The Need for Authority

In this connection it is worth noting that young children are quite satisfied with an assured and authoritative reply even if it is couched in terms that they cannot be expected to understand. For example, if a five-year-old asks "Who made God?" the answer can be: "Nobody made God. He was always there. It is God who made everything else." That is all. When, later on, he faces a logical problem and says, "But surely someone must have made God—he couldn't have just happened" his mind will be sufficiently stretched to take in the answer: "Well, suppose somebody *did* make God—there's still the question, who made that Somebody? You can go on like that for ever, unless you get back to a God who was always there." I would even go a step further and say: "That's why we call God the First Cause—the one who caused everything else, but was not caused himself"—adding "Never mind if you don't get that —it's the truth just the same, and later on, if you study a bit of philosophy, you'll find it easier to grasp." That is the kind of authoritative reply that even quite young children will accept with confidence. There is no harm in their realizing that there are aspects of truth beyond their grasp. As Baron von Hügel once said: "One of the first things Tommy must understand is that there are some things Tommy will *never* understand." It is when we try vainly to water down great truths with the idea of making them "comprehensible" to children that we are in danger of undermining their confidence and fostering doubts. A mother once asked me: "How am I to explain the Trinity to my little boy of five?" The answer is: You don't "explain" the Trinity to a five-year-old. You just tell him that God is Father, Son, and Holy Spirit, and leave it, for the time being, at that. Later on you may give him various pictures and analogies which will help him to see that the Trinity is a *reasonable* idea, though nothing will ever "explain" it even to the most profound philosopher. Often this kind of despairing appeal merely reflects doubts in the mind of the parent. They are all at sea because their own

faith is not secure. That is why the authoritative answer—
the answer of Christ's Church—is always the best for a
young child, though (as I have said) we must deliberately
prepare ourselves for the time when his questions will
become more penetrating and logical. When that time
comes, if we don't know the answer ourselves, we may
sometimes be wise to go to the expert; to say, "Let's go and
ask the Vicar about that" and then to go together. Even
then, we must encourage the child not to expect easy
potted answers. When a boy of ten once asked me, "How
does the crucifixion of Jesus really save us from our sins?"
I felt bound to reply: "I can't answer that question in two
minutes. You will have to be prepared to do some hard
thinking about it." He agreed, and we later spent the
better part of an hour building up a picture which helped
the boy to find, within the limits of his experience, a satisfying reply. He was left with the realization that there
was still plenty more thinking to be done!

8. *Father Christmas*

It is impossible to discuss the problem of children's questions and their whole approach to religion without saying
something about Father Christmas. It is extraordinary how
many children come to confuse Father Christmas with God
and have to face an acute readjustment of all their ideas
when they discover that Father Christmas is only an attractive "myth". In fact, Father Christmas has very much the
same kind of dangers as some of the mythical things we
are tempted to tell children about sex. A woman once wrote
to me, in connection with the B.B.C. "Silver Lining" programme: "I have lost God. . . . When I found out about
Father Christmas all my religion lost its thrill." I was surprised to discover from many other listeners' letters what
a common experience this is. It is an obvious danger and

one we must be on our guard against. Children very easily come to regard Father Christmas and the Christmas story itself as all of a piece, and the disillusionment that comes when they "find out" about Father Christmas, or some older child scornfully enlightens them, may often produce a bitter reaction against God and strike at the roots of their faith. This is no light matter and does indeed require careful and imaginative handling. For this reason I suggest that it is a mistake to let children go on "believing" in Father Christmas too long. It is a delightful fantasy while they are very young, when children live in a world of fantasy and do not make a clear distinction between fantasy and fact; but when they reach the age of five or six and are beginning to become literal-minded and realistic they should be helped to realize that Father Christmas is not the same kind of "truth" as God the Father, but is simply a pictorial way of, so to speak, dramatizing the spirit of Christmas. Like all poetic expression, it is essential truth enshrined in a symbol, but they should never be allowed to go on confusing the symbol with the reality. In my experience children will quite happily accept this explanation without forfeiting any of the sheer delight of Christmas. They will still go on joyfully hanging up their stockings to see what Santa Claus will bring! But they will be saved from that kind of acute disillusionment which may involve a painful unsettling of their simple faith. A child who is not helped to make this important distinction between fact and fantasy at the proper moment will be tempted to regard the Story of Bethlehem (which is the core of all our Christian belief) as all part of a childish fantasy which adults outgrow. They will throw away the baby with the bathwater! This is a far more fruitful cause of religious doubt than we often realize and one we need to be very much aware of.

9. *Fears and Bogeys*

Then there is that other matter I spoke of at the beginning of this chapter—the child's tendency to make quite alarming bogeys out of simple misunderstandings, often purely verbal ones. That is another thing we need to watch continually. We can never hope to anticipate every possible misconception, but we can become so sensitive to the way a child's mind works that we can at any rate go to some trouble to ensure that as far as possible he understands what we are trying to say. The "Banana Houses" I quoted is a typical example of verbal misunderstanding, though not a very serious one. Others may be more serious. For me, that phrase "the Wrath of God" is still saturated with a sense of dislike tinged with dread because at a very early age, I was somehow allowed to get the idea that thunder and lightning and earthquakes were expressions of God's violent anger and that he used such things to strike down people who annoyed him. Fortunately I got over that, but for many people this sort of early misimpression may result later in a positive hatred of all that religion stands for. So we must watch closely the meaning our children attach to words and ideas, and be careful, if we can, to check any growing misconceptions. I know one small boy who reacted violently against the thought of "God the Holy Ghost", because the word "ghost" for him meant a terrifying spectre and he had a hard struggle to dissociate this fear from his picture of God. He found the term Holy Spirit more palatable. We can all think of cases of such childish misunderstanding, some of them quite trivial—the sort of things that make amusing "schoolboy howlers"; but my point is that the child's readiness to twist the meaning of words into fears and bogeys has its very serious side and we cannot be too much on our guard to ensure that we never say things—or do things—that are liable to create false ideas or tensions in his mind, and that we must be always on the watch to deal reassuringly with the false ideas he is bound to come by anyway.

One of the most terrible instances of the kind of false idea which can haunt a child's life and devastate his religion is described by C. S. Lewis in his book *Surprised by Joy*.[1] When he was a schoolboy his prayer life was dominated by a fear (picked up in some obscure way) that unless he concentrated his mind on every single word of his prayers with undivided attention, he was somehow incurring God's anger and vengeance. Sometimes he would kneel for hours at his bedside in an agony of spirit, going through the same prayers over and over again, so as to be sure that he had not fallen into the grievous sin of allowing his mind to wander. It is a shattering picture of a quite needless self-torture, and any grown-up person who had been in close touch with his developing prayer life could in a few words have dispelled this horror. It is not every child who recovers his spiritual balance after such a shocking experience.

A friend of mine once related to me a similar experience of his early childhood. He had been taught to believe that our Lord's Second Coming might take place at any moment of the day or night and that, in that moment, the "saved" would be caught up with Christ into heaven and the "damned" would be left behind to their fate, which had been depicted for him in the most terrifying terms. One sunny afternoon, when he was a very young child, he came home from school to find the house empty and deserted and the street uncannily quiet. He was overwhelmed with panic. With the unreasoning certainty of a child, he *knew* that our Lord had come again and that he had been left behind. The shock that he suffered then—even though it lasted only a short while, till his mother, who had been called away by a neighbour, returned to console him—was

[1] C. S. Lewis, *Surprised by Joy* (Geoffrey Bles), p. 63f.

so profound that in middle life it still affected him with the quality of a nightmare. Here is an instance of how considered and deliberate teaching, which did not involve any real misconceptions on the part of the child, led to quite needless distress and may have had disastrous consequences. The consequences in any case were serious enough. We might well question whether such ideas, however much they may be to us a matter of conviction, can be safely instilled into a child's immature mind without producing fears and conflicts which may in the long run merely defeat our purpose in teaching them. Ideas associated with Judgment, Hell, and Damnation need to be handled with infinite care and should never be pictured at all outside the context of God's fatherly love and compassion for all human souls.[1]

So, in answering children's questions and forestalling their early misconceptions, it is always best to let the emphasis of all our teaching be on the love of God and his infinite care and concern for our highest welfare. Let the compassionate figure of our Lord dominate the whole scene, without losing sight of the strength and challenge of it. But all the terminology of wrath and vengeance can well be left over till the child is old enough to interpret it in a spiritual sense. Phrases like "hellfire" or "washed in the blood of the lamb" are poetical and analogical expressions of very real truths, but until those truths are within his spiritual grasp a child will inevitably visualize them in vivid material pictures which may vitiate his whole experience of religion.

Summary

We have tried again to look at broad sweeping principles

---

[1] For a powerful account of a child's reactions to this kind of teaching, all Christian parents and teachers of religion should read *Father and Son*, by Edmund Gosse.

rather than at details, because a grasp of principles is always the best approach to practical problems. To summarize, our answers to children's questions should be guided by the following four rules:

(1) They should preserve the true character of God, as revealed in Jesus Christ.

(2) They should be reassuring (as they cannot avoid being if they are soundly rooted in Christian verities).

(3) They should be strictly and essentially "true" within the limits imposed by the child's immature understanding.

(4) If you don't know the answer, admit it—and then go and look for it, with the child's help.

7

Children and the Church

So far we have been concerned almost entirely with the child's earliest experiences of religion in the life of the family _at home_, which means chiefly his private prayers and the general spirit and atmosphere of home life from which he drinks in his first formative impressions. We must be quite realistic about this and recognize, with regret, that we have been contemplating an ideal picture of how these things may happen in a Christian home; because the number of homes where anything even approaching this is being attempted is likely for a long time to remain pitifully small.

9. The Church's Claim at Baptism

But nevertheless this ideal picture contains the challenge with which the Church, through her priests and leaders, and not least through the contacts of practising Christian parents with non-practising ones, must be constantly confronting people, especially the people who bring their babies week by week to our fonts for Baptism. The most vital point of contact with all parents (specially young ones) is through their concern for their children's welfare, and we shall find them very ready to accept this kind of suggestion if it is made urgently and sympathetically on all possible occasions, more especially in preparation for marriage and in preparation for the baptism of their babies. At such times, when they are accepting a gift conferred by the Church, they are open to the Church's guidance, particularly when we can help them to realize that their own personal integrity is deeply involved, as well as the spiritual wellbeing of

most vital pt. 1.

their children. In every possible way—through the Mothers' Union and Young Wives' Groups, through Confirmation talks and sermons, through Marriage preparation and Churchings and Baptism interviews, and through normal pastoral visitation—these practical concerns should be made constantly and freshly alive to our people. Within the Church itself, there are thousands of parents hungering for this kind of guidance; and all the time our routine pastoral contacts are giving invaluable openings with thousands more who both need and welcome it. I would go so far as to suggest that the parish priest might make this whole approach to children (with all the many practical activities it involves) the basis of all pastoral visitation where families of young children are concerned. He need then never be at a loss for a topic of conversation—and one in which the Church can take a powerful initiative! It might well be adopted as a deliberate and sustained policy which will gain all the more force from continual repetition.

But it is not only the parish priest upon whom this urgent task is laid. All Christian people must be equally alive to it and informed about it, so that, whether in casual conversation with neighbours who are arranging to bring their babies for Baptism, or in the more formal contacts provided by visiting infants on the Cradle Roll or children absent from Sunday School, they can be constantly bringing these ideals to the notice of the parish at large. More general and diffuse talk about religion seldom impresses the outsider very much. It is only when religious concern can be crystallized into a practical challenge profoundly affecting their children's upbringing and answering the question "What can I do about it?" that they may be drawn to listen and become (to use a term popular in America) "involved".

I have thought it necessary to pause here and offer that comment, because, as we now go on to consider the process of bringing a child into the worshipping life of the Church, we shall find ourselves faced with the same dilemma—that most of what I want to say will appear to apply immediately only to the *Christian* family and will represent the ideal approach. But the same is true of this as of all that we have considered so far; it comprises the kind of activity that we should teach emphatically to those who come to receive the Church's ministrations and which, I suggest, <u>we have the moral right to require of them as the fulfilment of the solemn vows they undertake before God at the font on their children's behalf</u>. The response may not be immediate and will certainly not be universal; but to challenge people, with the full weight of the Church's authority, may prove the most potent way of awakening their conscience; and any parish priest who has taken this course with firmness and sympathy (recognizing that he is contending against several generations of laxity for which the Church is almost entirely to blame, and that therefore he is bound to meet with a certain understandable resistance) has discovered that parents here and there, though in increasing numbers, have found themselves impelled to examine the reality of their own religion and (if only for the sake of their children) to make a new beginning. We shall consider the problem of the purely pagan home in the next chapter. This chapter will be concerned with the kind of approach that would seem to be ideal for any Christian home, or for one that wanted to accept the ideal. We pass on then to consider the place and training of children in the life of the Christian Community, the Church of Christ.

B. *Corporate Religion*

In this country we need to be constantly stressing the *corporate* obligations of the Christian religion, because <u>it is a peculiarly British characteristic to regard religion as an entirely personal and private affair</u>—"What a man does

with his solitariness". It is commonly expressed in the view
that it is possible to be a "good Christian" without bother-
ing about the Church at all, and so it will be valuable to
make a clear statement about that before we proceed further.
Our Lord never once gave encouragement to the idea of
"lone" Christians, living good and moral lives in complete
isolation. To him the whole conception of God's children
as a "Family", sharing a common life and responsibility,
was absolutely central. The life and worship of the Body
of Christ is an integral part of the Gospel, quite inseparable
from the total practice of religion. We cannot too often
remind people (especially parents) that religion is much
more than ethical training, or even personal aspiration and
prayer. It is full participation in the worship, witness, and
warfare of the Church of Christ. It was Christ who gave
us the Church as we know it—it is God's creation, not
man's—and he told us that we can find life as God means
it to be only within the fold of the Church. In fact, the
Church is not merely a group of like-minded individuals
deciding to band together into a "society" for furthering
their particular interests. You can join or leave that kind
of society just as you please, as you happen to find yourself in sympathy or out of sympathy with its purposes. But
you cannot do that with the Church. The Church (as we
have seen) is a community of people who share, not merely
common aims and ideals, but the power of a common life
—the very life of God himself. When you become a member
of the Church (by Baptism) it is not like adding another
apple to a basket of apples, where each apple still preserves its separate identity and is just one of an aggregate;
it is like grafting another apple on to an apple tree, so that
the life of the tree flows into it, and its individual existence
(though still preserved) is merged in the total life of the
tree. That is what happens to every baby at his Baptism.
He is grafted into the Church of God, the Body of Christ,

8   103

and the very life and power of God flow into him. The life and worship of the Church are absolutely central in Christianity. However good our home training may be, however upright and moral our life, we can never be true Christians outside the Church; and we can never bring up our children as true Christians outside it either.

Prob. today

This is a truth barely acknowledged by the thousands of people who bring their children to our fonts for Baptism. It is our duty not only to teach them this truth and to require of them practical recognition of it, but also to provide within our church life the kind of setting that will help and encourage people to discharge these obligations with some hope of success. There are far too many churches of all persuasions in which the care and teaching of the children is a mere department, isolated and divorced from the interest and sympathy of the worshipping congregation at large. Jesus took a little child and set him *in the midst*—and that is the true place of the child in the concerns of the Christian community. We shall have to consider this more fully when we deal later with the responsibility of the Church as a whole. Meanwhile we must confine our attention for the moment to the responsibility of the parents for their children's upbringing within the Family of the Church.

C. *Promises at the Font*

The child in his baptism is made a member of Christ—as completely a member as any other baptized Christian, however advanced or exalted—and from that moment onwards our business must be to help him to learn and understand what this membership in the Body of Christ involves, so that he may assume step by step the responsibilities of it. This process of teaching (which will go on side by side with his personal training in prayer) is meant to ensure his recognition and acceptance of something already done. His

Baptism has conferred on him an indelible character. Nothing can ever alter it. It may be obscured by ignorance or overwhelmed by indifference, but it remains—the child has received the gift of the Holy Spirit and is incorporated into the divine society. From then onwards the whole purpose of his training, *vis-à-vis* the Church, is to make sure that he grows up knowing and understanding the nature of this status conferred in baptism, the responsibilities that it carries with it (undertaken on his behalf by his godparents), and the obligation laid upon him to make his own choice about it when he reaches an age of discretion.

It is clear that, in the Anglican formularies, Baptism is not regarded as properly completed without Confirmation; and therefore the obligation implicit in the promises of the godparents is that the child shall be carefully taught the Christian Faith within the life of the Christian Church until he is sufficiently instructed to be able to take upon himself, in Confirmation, the responsibility for his own spiritual life. Anything less than that is a violation of the solemn vows made to God at the font, and this truth must be brought home with the greatest possible emphasis to all who undertake to act as sponsors. At present sponsorship is still too commonly regarded as an empty formality and the choice of godparents (regardless of their own Christian profession) as largely a favour conferred. It is not surprising that so few take it seriously and the children drift away by the thousand. The remedy lies in our own hands and it will be to our eternal discredit to allow this state of things to continue unchecked.

So, I repeat, the purpose of all training which relates to the Church must be to help him recognize and accept a status already conferred which carries all the obligations of Church membership. The task of Christian teachers would be greatly lightened if every member of the Church would acknowledge this simple fact. And the process is the same in principle as with the child's training in personal religion —to put him into the kind of situation in which he can experience the corporate side of religion as an attractive and "grown-up" thing.

His share in the corporate life of the Church has actually begun with his Baptism. What can we do in those very early stages of his life to make this increasingly real to him?

D. *Growing up in the Church*

The most compelling way (as in all education) is by deliberately associating our teaching with some fascinating activity. It is a thousand pities that we have allowed religion to become so dull and unattractive to children. To a Jewish child religion was packed with excitement, colour, and activity. There were so many things to watch and take part in and ask questions about. These included, for example, the Passover, when the youngest child present always asked the question "What mean ye by this service?", a service which was a dramatic representation of that first hurried and exciting flight from the bondage of Egypt; the Feast of Tabernacles, which involved camping out under the stars, living in improvised "booths" made of branches, with all the joys of the open air and the campfire; a boy's first visit to Jerusalem for the Passover, involving a long and dangerous journey in good company and coming to its climax in all the solemn ritual of the Temple worship. It is right that children (not to say adults) should find religion enthralling, and Catholic worship has always tried to preserve in its feasts and fasts and colourful pageantry (possessing all the quality of drama) those pictorial and imaginative aspects which make such a powerful appeal to any child, as well as to grown-up people who do not "lose their fairylands". Far from being suspicious of these compelling aids to the imagination, we should make every possible use of them as we lead children into the life of the Church; we may even invent some of our own, as I suggested when I described the kind of "prayer corner" we can provide for our private prayer-times. Anything that arouses a child's fascinated interest is an invaluable aid.

For example, we may help a child from the earliest days to become aware of the importance of his Baptism by making the anniversary the occasion for some small family festivity. It need not be anything large and expensive, or compete in any way with his ordinary birthday. In large families that would in any case probably be unmanageable. But it will mean a lot to him if his Baptism Day—his spiritual Birthday, so to speak—can be treated as an outstanding event in his life. It could be marked by a small gift, or a special cake, or an outing, or a little friend to tea —anything that will kindle his interest and help him to accept his baptism, and ask questions about it, as naturally as he accepts his birthday. In this way his membership of the Church of Christ will come to be associated in his mind with a number of happy memories—and that is the kind of thing which determines far more than we often realize a child's later response to the claims of religion.

Baptism Day [margin note]

E. *Visiting the Church*

Then next (I am still speaking about the infant who is not yet old enough for Sunday school) it is important to let him become familiar with the inside of the church long before he ever goes to an act of public worship. Here again —as with his private prayers—there is no need to wait till he becomes obviously aware and observant. It often happens that a child is never taken inside a church after his Baptism, until at the age of three or four (or generally very much later) his parents may take him rather tentatively to an "adult" service; and then the likelihood is that he will find it all very strange and forbidding. Let him get used to

Prob. [margin note]

visiting the church from his babyhood. From time to time, while he is still in his pram, mother can get into the habit of dropping into church for a few minutes, on the way to the shops or the park, and taking the baby with her. She can do so regularly once or twice a week (perhaps even daily) as part of the normal routine. As the baby becomes more wakeful she can carry him into the church in her arms and sit with him quietly for a few minutes before the altar and then finish by kneeling (still with the baby in her arms) and saying a short prayer aloud. He will gain a lot from that simple experience of using a church. As he grows older these regular visits will give opportunities for wandering around the church and looking at things. Let him visit the font where he was christened, the lectern and the pulpit, the pictures and the windows and, at the heart of everything, the altar. As you answer his inevitable questions you are giving him step by step a happy and natural familiarity with God's house which will make it much easier for him later on to find his own place in it; and always finish such visits by kneeling together and saying a short prayer, preferably aloud.

One of the most memorable outings my two older children had, when they were very small, was when the vicar of the parish where we lived for a while (who understood small children very well) made a businesslike appointment with them beforehand (booking the date with a flourish in his diary and driving up in his car to fetch them at the appointed time), for a visit to the church. It was a mixture of a state visit and a conducted tour! He showed them everything, telling them all about the saints in the windows, letting them wind up the font cover and play a few discords on the organ and peep into all the mysterious corners. He took them into the vestries and explained the vestments and the sacred vessels. It was something they never forgot—and from that moment onwards it was *their* church and they loved every bit of it. That is another instance of what I was speaking about in the last chapter—giving a child an experience of religion which is happy and reassuring and adult, and which makes him feel that he belongs to it and that it belongs to him.

F. *Going to Services*

This kind of thing can be done—and done regularly—long before a child is normally responsive enough to be taken to a service. In fact, many people are apprehensive about taking children to church services too young in case they develop an early distaste which may later be difficult to eradicate. This is a very real danger, and on the whole it is wiser to err on the side of caution rather than haste. As long as the child is being given these regular opportunities of finding himself at home inside a church in his own way we need not be in too big a hurry to introduce him to public worship. On the other hand, where suitable conditions exist, many people would be in favour of taking even tiny babies to public services of the church. Later on we will consider the opportunities that a good Parish Eucharist affords for this very early participation in adult worship. Where there is an atmosphere of profound devotion and *koinonia*, and where children are made welcome without a hint of superiority or undue repression, we need never hesitate to allow the tiniest children to share such worship. As with everything else, they will catch the spirit of worship from people who are really worshipping. But where there is any danger of a child encountering an atmosphere of restraint, boredom, or even positive misbehaviour and irreverence on the part of older people, it would be far wiser to delay; because, as we have reminded ourselves repeatedly, it is the general impression he receives, whether free and happy or dull and oppressive, which will colour his whole attitude to the Church and her worship. I may offer the hint here (which we will develop more fully later) that probably the best service for a young child is a good sung Eucharist, where the singing and movement and colour can appeal to his imagination without straining his understanding. (Many will feel, as I do, that a Service like Matins is largely unsuitable for young children because it demands a degree of mental concentration of which children are not yet capable.) But don't be unduly worried if he fidgets—a young child must be always moving his body and it is not a sign of irreverence. If you take your own part in the service quietly and without fuss—and if other grown-up people can be persuaded to do the same—it will teach him a lot more than any amount of exhortation and regimenting.

G. The Family at Church

The ideal thing, wherever possible, is to go to church as a family. The most powerful influence you can exert on a child's growing understanding of the corporate life of the Church is to let it be assumed, quite casually and without argument, that we all go to church together. If ever, for one reason or another, he shows any disinclination to go, this unspoken assumption will be a more powerful incentive than any form of persuasion. Young children are very conventional. They like to do the things other people do, especially if they are allowed an air of privilege and grown-up-ness. But remember that, although he will agree to come with you, he will soon begin to rebel against being sent. Children go more readily where we lead from the front than where we push from behind—and in this they are really no different from the rest of the human race! In these days, when Mother so often finds it difficult to get to church on Sunday mornings (at least where services remain at the long-hallowed but rather inconvenient hour of eleven) it might well become the accepted function of Father to lead the family in this respect. But the ideal thing—and one

which the Parish Eucharist makes increasingly possible—
is for the whole family to worship regularly together. Then,
in the same way as with private prayers, rebellion is less
likely to raise its head, and if it does it will be more readily
overcome by the force of family custom.

It is true that many Christian congregations will need to
undergo a revolutionary change in their whole conception
of worship before the presence of young children will be
readily welcomed among them. This is a difficulty we shall
examine more fully in a later chapter. But since the child is,
by his Baptism, a privileged member of the Christian
Family, we ought not to countenance any longer the kind
of intolerance which would seek to exclude him or to mini-
mize his importance. For my own part, I have always
deprecated the custom, in some churches, of segregating
the children, herding them together in a gallery or a remote
corner, under martial supervision, in case they should disturb the maturer devotions of the elderly! There is
obviously a proper place for special children's services and
instructions, but, as far as the corporate worship of the
whole Christian Family is concerned, I believe it is important that children should be allowed to take their place quite
naturally and by right in what they may come to accept as
a family affair. "Young men and maidens, old men and
children, praise the name of the Lord"—that is the true
picture of the Church at worship.

H. *"For Children only"?* luring audy to Williams

This in its turn may throw a searching light on the
much-debated topics of the *Children's Church*, the
Children's Corner, the *Children's Eucharist*, and all other
special concentrations on children that tend to isolate them
from the rest of the "family" and emphasize their immaturity. There are many ways in which their needs must
be met separately, but I would most seriously question (for

the reasons we have discussed above) whether the corporate worship of the Christian Family is one of them. It is impossible to be dogmatic about this, but we may find some guidance in the fact that children themselves actually prefer to do things with grown-up people when they are given the opportunity and encouraged to do so. They don't like being constantly reminded of their childish limitations. They like to feel grown-up. The Children's Corner, with its special books and pictures, may sometimes serve a useful purpose in a large and barren church; though it is significant that so many attractive Children's Corners have a bewildering air of being "laid on" and very little used! If the whole church were as picturesque and fascinating as it ought to be, children could readily be helped to use it as grown-up people do; and they are likely to be more deeply impressed by its long vistas and open spaces and dignified sanctuaries than by some small and confined corner devoted to their particular needs (so often misconceived by adults). Children's Corners are often advocated on the ground that small children are intimidated by the mere size and emptiness of a great church and need a homely focus. From my own observations I would doubt the truth of this. I have known small children gasp with delight at the majestic vistas of a great cathedral; and a church need never be overpowering to any child who is allowed to catch the spirit of wonder and reverence from his earliest infancy in the way I have tried to describe. But there may indeed still be a place for the small chapel or the quiet corner, as long as it is not labelled specifically "for children only". With the principles underlying the *Children's Church* and the *Children's Eucharist* we are on safer ground in questioning their wisdom, because there we have the kind of isolation which makes a division in the family just at the very point where, I suggest, it should be most completely at one. The offering of the Eucharist is the offering of the whole Church; and I can only express my personal conviction that children will grow up more naturally into their heritage of worship and their service of the Church if from the outset they can be welcomed, so to speak, on an equal footing with the rest of God's family.

Special Teaching

We have been thinking (again largely in terms of general principles) about the child's introduction into the corporate life of the Church rather than about his actual instruction in the faith; but side by side with this (and not as a substitute for it) he should be going to Sunday School or some other suitable instruction, so that he may fill out this experience of worship with the knowledge and understanding proper to his age. But this instruction can only have real value in so far as it is helping the child all the time to appropriate the Christian Religion, not merely as a set of theological ideas, but also as a life of prayer, worship, and service, within the setting of the Christian community. Stories about Old Testament heroes or the missionary journeys of St Paul—even the Gospel stories themselves, combined with a full teaching of Christian ethical standards—will not be enough to hold him unless at the same time he is learning to take his place as an active member of Christ's Church.

Full Membership

So all the activity and training we have been discussing —his private life of prayer and his experience of public worship, together with his instruction in the faith at Sunday School and Day School—must all come to a focus in one definite objective: that he should become a full practising member of the Church as soon as possible. This is no place to enter fully into the much disputed question of the proper age for Confirmation. Much will depend on the child's own character and gifts, his home circumstances, and the nature of the particular congregation in which he grows up, as well as the general social setting of his life. Many priests who work in industrial areas will feel (as I do) that the sooner a child is confirmed and becomes set in good habits of prayer, penance, and communion before the stress of adolescence sets in, the more likely he is to be armed against the dangers and stresses of the industrial world when he leaves school at fifteen. It is in any case highly doubtful whether adolescence itself, with its emotional upheaval, is a suitable time for Confirmation; and where it cannot come earlier it is probably better that it should wait until the stress of adolescence has subsided, although by that time many promising young people have already been lost to the Church. It is worth noting that the Prayer Book clearly envisages Confirmation as soon as a child reaches the age of discretion (it actually says as soon as he can repeat the Creed, the Lord's Prayer, and the Ten Commandments, and has been instructed in the Catechism —which does not suggest a very advanced age!); and my own firm conviction is that a boy or girl should ideally be "promoted" to full Church membership and the Sacraments before the tensions of adolescence begin. This will give him the spiritual support and the sense of stability he most needs at that time.

I realize that this raises the problem of "conversion"; but with children conversion ought never to be strongly emotional experience. A child's religion (as indeed all religion) is largely a matter of the will, not of the emotions. As soon as he understands the difference between right and wrong, broadly conceived, and recognizes the need for God's help (or "Grace"), and is prepared in good faith to offer his life to God and try to serve him, then he is ready for the full sacramental life of the Church; and he will find it an immense strength to be already settled in regular habits of spiritual discipline before the temptations of the world press too hardly on him. But these are personal reflections, reinforced by my own particular experience of children and young people chiefly in industrial and artisan areas, and there will continue to be wide divergences of opinion about these problems. One thing is certain—and it is the climax of all we have been considering—that the child's whole approach to God through prayer and public worship must come to an issue at the earliest possible moment in Confirmation and Communion.

One final word. In the last resort, as I have continually stressed, our most powerful influence over our children is not what we say but what we are and do. There is an old saying, "I cannot hear what you *say*, because what you *are* is shouting so loudly". That is the whole thing in a nutshell. If my own life is deeply rooted in prayer and worship and sacrament, then my influence on my children (even if it is not as immediate and obvious as I should like) will bear fruit in God's good time. "For their sakes I consecrate myself."

8

The Church's Care for her Children

IN all that we have considered in the previous chapters the
focus has been on the responsibility of the parents for the
religious training of their children, both in personal prayer
and public worship. It has been in many ways an ideal
picture, almost a counsel of perfection; but it is by setting
the highest possible standard that we may most hopefully
present to people at large the enormous claims that the
education of children lays upon all who have "the care and
nurture" of them. It would be unrealistic to suppose that,
at any rate for a long time to come, we shall see this kind
of thing happening in more than a handful of Christian
households in any parish; but at least we may have a right
to expect that instructed Christian parents may give careful
thought to their children's training along these lines. From
them these concerns may then spread to families on the
fringe of the Church's life and even beyond, and become
in time a "leaven that leaveneth the whole lump". But that
can only happen as their conviction deepens into a missionary zeal. For far too long the Church has had no clear
policy for the care of her children. It has been all too hap-
hazard and uninformed, and left largely to goodwill and
chance. A clear, consistent policy based on recognizable
principles of the kind we have been outlining and sponsored by the parish priest will go far towards reducing the
chaos to order.

But responsibility for the nurture of the children within
the Church does not rest only with the parents and the
parish priest, as so many good Church people fondly

imagine. In any case we have to recognize that a high proportion (probably something like ninety per cent) of the children who come at some time within the orbit of the Church's influence have a home background of virtual paganism, or at best lukewarm goodwill, and are not likely to get very much of the kind of help we have so far considered. This brings us face to face with one of the biggest problems of our times and one that lays a heavy burden of responsibility four-square on the shoulders of all professing members of the Christian Family.

The Child in the midst

Read again the incident reported in Matt. 18.2–6: "Jesus called a little child unto him, and set him in the midst of them." Is it unduly fanciful to see in that act a vivid object lesson which the Church has been all too slow to learn? Jesus called the child to come and stand side by side with him (an act of identification which on another occasion he made even more explicit in the words "Inasmuch . . .") and then he placed the child deliberately in the very centre of that company of twelve supremely important men, lifting him up into a place of conspicuous prominence as he said: "Whosoever receives a little child like this in my name is receiving me." This act was the occasion for some profound teaching about the true values of the Kingdom of God, but it is impossible to miss the force of it also as a simple acted parable. It surely proclaims beyond any possibility of mistaking that the proper place of the child in the care and concern of the Christian Church (and in practice that means the local congregation) is "in the midst". The Church's children must be the centre and focus of the Church's work.

No one could deny that the proper place of the child is in the midst. Today's children are tomorrow's Church. And yet pause and consider what is in actual practice the place of the children in the life of the Church at large—and of your church in particular. It is, taken generally, a gloomy picture. Think how the Church's care of her children has been too often allowed to degenerate into a mere subsidiary "department", the preserve (sometimes the jealous preserve) of a devoted few with special gifts or a sense of vocation—a department far too often divorced from the interest or care of the ordinary "church-goer". The very term "church-goer", we may note in passing, is a reproach and one we ought not to tolerate any longer; for it fosters the delusion that the Church of Christ is simply a place that people go to, like the cinema or the concert hall, instead of a divine society, the spirit-bearing Body, engaged in a holy war, with the obligation of ensuring that every member is trained and equipped for his share in the campaign. It is precisely because so many professing Christians are content to be "church-goers", without accepting their full responsibility as members of the Body of Christ, that the problem we are now discussing has ever come into being. I am sure our Lord would have been horrified if anyone had described him as a synagogue-goer! Merely to "go to church" without ever becoming involved in the Church's age-long care for human souls, which is part of her "worship" of God, is a blind and fruitless activity and a source of great weakness to the whole Body. This is the chief reason why the ordinary man in the pew often knows little and cares less about the Church's work with her children. The children must be taught, of course, but that is the business of the Sunday School, not *his* business; and the Sunday School is likely to be as remote from his interest as plans for educating the aborigines of Australia! He faintly despises Sunday School teachers. He thinks that the Church's children —if they are to be allowed to be present at public services at all, and even then only on sufferance—should be segregated in remote corners where their antics are least liable to interfere with his devotions. On the whole he would prefer to have them accommodated elsewhere. That is not an unfair picture of the kind of selfish obscurantism with which many of us are trying to contend. It is a bleak repudiation of our Lord's attitude to the lambs of the flock.

Where we are failing

The simple truth is that every baby baptized at the font of the parish church becomes immediately the inescapable concern and responsibility of every single member of the particular congregation—as well as of the Church at large. It is their duty and privilege to welcome him into the Family of which they are grown-up members and accept their share of concern for his future training. But too often this truth is hidden from them because they have never been encouraged to regard the Baptism of Infants as a matter that concerns them. It is not altogether their fault. They are the victims of an evil system which has been allowed to grow up during the past century; and when we are a little more enlightened we shall all begin to have a very uneasy conscience about our present custom of hole-and-corner baptisms, furtively performed at tea-time on Sundays, which can never appeal to anybody's imagination as a symbol of receiving a child into the congregation of Christ's flock. A resounding reform must begin at this point. The Prayer Book clearly requires that the Baptism of Infants (Public Baptism as distinct from Private Baptism in emergency) should be administered "when the most number of people come together", that the "congregation there present may testify the receiving of them that be newly baptized into the number of Christ's Church".

To ensure this publicity it also enjoins that Baptisms should take place at Morning or Evening Prayer. In earlier days that was possible, but with the advent of gas-lighting and the postponing of Evening Prayer from 3 p.m. to the popular hour of 6.30, Baptisms at Evening Prayer became less convenient and there gradually grew up the custom of baptizing babies on Sunday afternoons when no one was present except the parents, sponsors, and other friends of the child. This has become in our own time, when a high proportion of Baptism parties consist largely of infidels, a positive scandal; specially when (to add to the gravity of the situation) "sponsors" who make no profession of Christian belief, or who perhaps belong to some denomination not in communion with the Church of England, are allowed to take upon their lips (without a word of explanation or warning) solemn vows which they do not understand and have no intention of keeping. Quite often even the parents themselves see no need to be present at their child's baptism and leave it entirely to the godparents. No one who takes the trouble to examine this situation honestly (in the light of the Church's declared purpose) can possibly rest satisfied with it. It is a corruption on the very threshold of a child's spiritual life. But besides doing infinite damage to the persons (including the child) who are permitted to take part in such an empty mockery, it does irreparable damage to the whole Body of Christ, because it obscures from the faithful, the ones most deeply implicated in every Baptism, the fact that the child is being "received into the congregation of Christ's flock" and has become one of themselves, with all the duties and obligations towards him which that must demand of them. For while the Priest is repeating those tremendous words "*We* receive this child into the congregation of Christ's flock" (where the "we" is not the plural of honour but denotes the whole congregation) Christ's flock is blissfully and unconcernedly having its Sunday tea, all unaware of the tremendous thing that is being done in its name and the terrific responsibility that is being unloaded upon it!

c. *Putting it right*

How is Baptism to be restored again to its proper place of publicity in the face of the whole congregation, so that this note of "reception" into the Christian Family (with the accountability it carries with it) may once again be a genuine and not a counterfeit experience? Many experiments are being tried throughout the Church. In some parishes (where Baptisms are few) they may be administered again at Evensong, perhaps in place of the prayers after the Third Collect. But the evening is not a convenient time for young babies to be out of their cots, and where Baptisms are many and frequent this practice might become rather unwieldy. In parishes where the Parish Eucharist has been adopted, Baptism might occasionally be arranged to follow it, and the congregation which has just assembled round the altar be thus given the opportunity to express their "comm-union" by receiving new members into their fellowship.

Another possible solution is the Family Service—a regular monthly or six-weekly open service on Sunday afternoons for children and their parents and friends—at which the administration of Baptism can be the focus of interest. I have adopted this practice in my own church and it has met with the most heartening response. The earlier part of the service can be kept quite short and the chief thought of it focused on some aspect of what it means to be a "member of Christ, the child of God, and an inheritor of the Kingdom of Heaven". We then proceed to the font, where all the younger children are brought to the fore, and the older children and the rest of the congregation are invited to face westward and to gather round as closely as the seating permits, leaving a lane through which the priest can walk after each Baptism to the centre of the Church. It is a remarkable experience to gaze down from the steps of the font on to a sea of interested faces massed around in a solid phalanx. After each baby has been baptized the priest carries it down through the crowd into the body of the church and there, standing in the midst, he invites everybody, with their prayer books open, to say with him the words of reception: "We receive this child into the congregation of Christ's flock . . . ". He then returns to the font and the same procedure is repeated with each baby. One of the most moving aspects of this procedure is the homely and yet completely reverent way in which the children, as well as grown-ups, will express their delighted admiration of the baby as it is carried down among them—"Oh, isn't he lovely! God bless him." Somehow this simple act, without disturbing the atmosphere of solemnity, breaks through the barrier of mere formality and brings home to the congregation the idea that this baby now "belongs to us".

But, however the thing is done, there can be little dispute that it must be done *somehow*, and we may have to contemplate a radical change in our whole parochial programme in order to make it possible. Once it has been achieved, and fully public Baptism has become the rule rather than the exception, the priest is in a position to teach, with some hope of understanding and acceptance, the responsibility of the whole worshipping congregation to the new members of the flock. Without it, even the most elaborate system of Cradle Rolls and visits and birthday cards, undertaken by a few devoted souls who see the point, will not serve to break down the rigid indifference of the rest; but once this has become a recognized practice the right atmosphere has been created for everybody, except the most obstinate and obtuse, to grasp the point and begin to do something about it. Here is just another instance of what I have described as creating the kind of situation in which we can have some hope of success. It is useless to insist on the fulfilling of obligations (or even to talk about them in theory) unless we first provide a setting within which it is practicable to observe them. This obvious truth has cropped up several times in the course of our survey. It goes deep to the roots of many of our most baffling problems and may often serve as a guide when we are tempted to ask "Where on earth does one *begin* with this?"

The People's Part

Until this kind of situation is deliberately created we shall continue to face tremendous difficulty in persuading more than a small handful of the congregation that the children are their concern. But it still remains true and must be dinned into them by every means available! It is their responsibility to ensure that the children baptized at the font do not drift away and be lost to the life of the Church. It is their business to see that each child is taught the faith and comes eventually to take his due part in the worship and work of the whole Family. All this is their business—and there is no escaping this grave responsibility which is laid upon them by the very nature of the Church; and even if they may be allowed to delegate some of the practical discharge of this obligation to special people (such as Sunday School teachers and Club leaders) they can never for a moment relinquish their ultimate responsibility to God for the souls of these children. The Church's children are and must always be the loving care of every other member of the Family of God.

The kind of Baptism Service we have described (which does express in a strongly imaginative way the idea of a "family welcome") makes its impression not only on the congregation, but also on the people (mostly "fringers" and "outsiders") who bring their babies to the font. The dignity and importance of the occasion is visibly enhanced by the mere number of people of all ages who are present at it, and that in itself is an impressive witness. But it goes deeper. The more warm and friendly the welcome, the more such people may be drawn towards the fellowship of the Church on purely human grounds of goodwill. But above all it provides (as another example of the principle we defined just now) a setting within which we can teach parents and sponsors the nature of their vows and offer them some hope of keeping them.

E. *Instruction for Baptism:*

The minimum instruction the parish priest should give to parents and godparents in preparation for a Baptism would include the meaning of the child's incorporation into the Church through the gift of the Holy Spirit, with its accompanying gifts of forgiveness and grace, and the implications of the threefold promise of the sponsors. These two aspects represent God's gift and our response. The second—the obligations of the sponsors—can only be discharged by the simple expedient of ensuring that the child is taught by the Church to the point where he can accept (or repudiate) the challenge of confirmation. This means that he must come, when he is old enough, to a Church of England Sunday School (or other instruction)—and not to the Sunday School of some other denomination; and that he should come as a matter of obligation and not as a matter of condescension. The parents are not conferring a favour on the Church by sending their children to be taught; they are merely fulfilling (in the most nominal way) the promise they made to God when the children were baptized; and Baptism was only given on that quite plain condition. In fact the Baptism of infants was originally a concession to Christian parents only (adult Baptism would be the norm) and the wholesale baptism of the children of pagan families was never contemplated. The situation we face today is one in which ninety per cent of the parents who bring their babies to be baptized are only nominally

Christian and virtually pagan; though we can do no more than make the best of the situation until the tide of faith turns. Meanwhile we must at least insist with all the emphasis we can that Baptism carries those privileges and those commitments and use every possible means to bring it home effectively. If parents cannot be prevailed upon to *bring* their children to church (which is the ideal) they must at least make it possible for the Church to welcome them to her services and instructions, and this is precisely where the kind of Baptisms we have described, reinforced by all the visiting and after-care undertaken by a congregation that is obviously deeply concerned, can make a powerful impact on the pagan homes and offer some hope that our demands will not fall on deaf ears. Again, we shall have provided a setting within which the requirements begin to look friendly and reasonable—and that, supported by love and prayer, may have a great converting power on the most hardened unbeliever.

May I add a final suggestion that whenever a family leaves the parish they should always be commended by the incumbent to the vicar of the parish to which they move. People are greatly impressed by this kind of concern and it helps to emphasize the claim that the Church makes upon them. It may sometimes also serve to remind an incumbent of his duty and give him a welcome excuse to visit the new arrivals.

9

The Place of the Sunday School

WE have considered the responsibility of the whole congregation for the welfare and training of the Church's children up to the point where they can accept for themselves, in Confirmation, their full status as members of the Church. The child who belongs to a Christian home, although the active oversight of his training in prayer and worship will obviously rest largely with his own parents, must still be received and welcomed into the worshipping Family and helped in every way to feel that he "belongs"; because, even where families come to church together, there can nevertheless be an atmosphere of isolation and individualism which may make a child feel that he is only there on sufferance. In this respect the whole congregation (knit together in a true *koinonia*, a friendly and welcoming fellowship) must still show an interest in the children of Christian parents and not assume that, because the children are in good hands, they can remain indifferent to them. It is when children are helped in every way to feel that their presence gives people pleasure and their absence is noted, that they will find themselves drawn into the Church's life.

4. *Children of pagan homes:*

But with children from non-Christian homes this friendly interest will need even more deliberate expression. These children will find their most immediate point of contact with the Church through the Sunday School—and perhaps through week-night organizations appended to the Sunday

School. They may never, in the earlier stages, come to church at all; though, as we shall consider in the next chapter, every effort ought to be made to bring them into the normal services of worship and link them with the Christian Family. But for the most part the Church's care for them will have to be discharged through the work of the Sunday School. This underlines again the imperative need for every member of the worshipping congregation to accept the Sunday School as a matter of personal concern and interest, because the children of the Church are, and must always be, their responsibility. Nothing else that can be said or done about Sunday Schools can have its full weight until this fact is more widely acknowledged and (in modern jargon) "implemented". That is why we have laid so much stress on it. Where this truth is in fact recognized by the local congregation the Church flourishes and the future is hopeful; where it is not, the life of the Church is languishing—and though we may discover and lament other causes of the decline, this is the one that lies at the roots of them all. The Church cannot hope to recover her vitality until the welcoming and training of her children (in both Day and Sunday School) becomes once more the passionate interest of the worshipping community as a whole, and not just a specialized section of it.

It is within this important setting that we go on to consider the particular work of the Sunday School as part of the educational function of the whole Church. We will consider first the aim of Sunday School teaching, and then inquire in what practical ways it may become a greater concern of all Church members.

The Purpose of Sunday Schools

The Book of Common Prayer (as we have already seen) makes it quite plain that all the teaching and training of children has one purpose only—to bring them into a living

127

and loving relationship with our Lord within the sacramental fellowship of the Church. It is not just a question of teaching Bible stories or moral precepts—or even the Catechism. A child will see very little point in all this information and will very soon forget it, unless he is learning to put it all into practice by becoming (as early as possible) a full active member of the worshipping body. Naturally he must be taught the Faith; but we need to remember (and to be constantly reminding him too) that it is bound to remain sterile and dull unless he is having a living experience of it.[1]

A recent Report published by the University of Leeds Institute of Education, dealing with an investigation into the religious beliefs of adolescents, showed that, by the age of seventeen, boys and girls retain practically nothing of the religious teaching given in Day or Sunday School unless they come from a Christian home or have kept some connection with a church. This ought not to surprise us. Christianity is a way of life, not a "subject" in the curriculum; and both Day Schools and Sunday Schools must recognize that mere "religious knowledge", unrelated to the worship and warfare of the Church and the practice of living, is as valueless as giving boys theoretical talks about football without ever letting them come within a mile of a football pitch! The rules of the game can only become significant (or even interesting) when you are actually learning to play it.

So one of the first things that the Sunday School (as well as the Day School) must obviously do is to acknowledge

[1] "Religious Education is education in Religion; not merely in theory, but also in practice. . . . It is hoped that the atmosphere of School worship and the new approach to religious instruction will increasingly lead children to become and remain full members of a worshipping community outside the School. If it does not, we should judge that, as religious education, it has failed." (Preface to *Lindsay Agreed Syllabus*.)

its own limitations. It must never be regarded (as it still is in some parts of England) as an end in itself; as a self-sufficient community—sometimes in actual competition with the parent Church—to which children may belong without any obligation of accepting the full status of church membership. The Sunday School is only one of the functions of the Church itself, not a substitute for it; and it is doing its work properly only as it brings more and more children into the normal worship of the whole congregation, specially at the Eucharist. The ideal of Christian worship (as we have noted) is a community, a true family of young and old, offering their praise to God in unison; and far from deprecating the presence of children at Church services we should in fact expect it and even (where circumstances permit) require it. The Sunday School has not completed its task till every child committed to its care has become a full, communicating member of the Church.

2. The Sunday School and the Congregation

In what ways can the congregation as a whole be expected to accept its due share of responsibility for this work?

First, the Church must concern itself officially with the work of the Sunday School and subsidiary organizations through the Parochial Church Council. This kind of official sponsorship will prove the best way of fostering and expressing, through the accredited representatives of the whole church electorate, the duty of the congregation at large; because such official sanction gives importance and dignity to the matter and inspires a growing respect for it, besides focusing it into a practical issue. The Church Council, by appointing a children's sub-committee with wide powers, should keep itself constantly informed about the progress of all the Church's work among children. It should be prepared to vote the largest possible sum of money to buy books and pictures and apparatus, and should regard the needs of the Sunday Schools as the first and not (as too often happens) the last claim on available funds. It is important that the Sunday Schools should be regarded as a charge on church expenses, figuring prominently in the official budget, and not a department that is expected to support itself out of the proceeds of its own collections! The Council should also interest itself vigorously in the premises (whether church or parish hall) in which the schools are held, recognizing the simple educational truth that children learn more through atmosphere than through instruction, and that dirty, dingy, or disorderly surroundings may infect them with an attitude of distaste or disdain which will later poison their whole religious outlook. A cheerful coat of paint in the church hall may be a much higher priority than a new frontal for the Lady Chapel! In this kind of way a Church Council can both encourage and express the whole church's responsibility for the teaching of the children.

Then the ordinary members of the congregation may be given positive opportunities of accepting a practical share in the work. Many of them, who have no special aptitude for teaching, might be prepared to visit regularly the babies on the Baptism Roll, keeping close touch with the parents, and so reminding them constantly of the promises they made at the font, until the children are old enough to come to Sunday School. They may also undertake to visit absentees and thus relieve some of the pressure on the teachers. Others, with practical or artistic gifts, might be willing to make charts and models and other such apparatus for the Sunday Schools, thus saving unnecessary expenditure and also assisting teachers who may not possess these aptitudes. They could be present at the teachers' preparation class and make invaluable contributions to the success of the lessons. Others again might help children from non-Christian homes to find their way into the fellowship of the Church by "sponsoring" a small number of children (perhaps only two or three)—calling for them, sitting with them in church, helping them to find their places and in general befriending them. For many a child whose parents never come to church this may become a real experience of "family worship". There is hardly any limit to the number of people who could undertake this simple act of service. Others again may feel able to take some small share in the children's weekday activities (a most vital part of the Church's contact with them), even if it is only boiling a kettle for canteen at a junior club, and so help to foster that sense of "belonging to a family" which is the keynote of Christian community. The mere presence of church people at the children's various organizations will create a powerful impression of interest to which children will warmly respond. Finally, there will be those who, in addition to such active interest or perhaps as a specific piece of service in itself, will undertake to pray regularly and systematically, by name and in detail, for the children and the teachers and all the varying needs of the whole work. A Prayer Group could also be formed for this purpose.

A "Sunday School Fellowship"

But these opportunities for the members of the congregation to show an active interest will need a certain amount of planning and management. People are often shy of offering to do these things, even when they would like to, for fear of being presumptuous. An effective way of creating an outlet for such service is to form some sort of "Sunday School Fellowship", open to all who are willing to help in any way. The membership can be unlimited and would comprise the teachers and all who will undertake to assist them as visitors, "sponsors", makers of apparatus, club-helpers, or intercessors. Such a Fellowship can meet quite informally at regular intervals and keep the whole situation under constant review. It will be an enormous encouragement to the teachers and break down the feeling of isolation they often have to endure. It can become a recruiting ground for talent of all kinds, as well as an occasion for social intercourse. Out of such a group all kinds of invaluable projects can emerge, almost spontaneously, and it will form the nucleus of a working party which can undertake to handle anything from a Sunday School outing to a "Home and Family" exhibition. In the first instance it may need to be hand-picked from among the keenest church members, but once it is well established it can become a pressure-group which will gradually exert a beneficial influence over the whole church, continually bringing in new people and making this challenge of corporate responsibility a living part of the church's whole witness.

E. *The Need for Efficiency*

Lastly, we must examine the educational quality of our Sunday Schools and the kind of teaching that is given in them. This brings us to the question of standards. Every care must be taken to ensure that the instruction given under the aegis of the Church can compare as favourably as possible with the highly qualified teaching normally given in day schools for the rest of the week. Children are learning their "secular" knowledge, for the most part, from skilled teachers who understand the value of attractive teaching aids and who can command the kind of discipline that is essential in the classroom. If, on Sundays, the child learns about God and the Church at the hands of some young and raw adolescent, unskilled in teaching, ignorant of method, and incapable of discipline, amid surroundings of dinginess and disorder, the implied contrast between the importance of secular and sacred knowledge will not be lost on him, as many have known to their cost. As we have said repeatedly, it is this kind of "impression" that shapes a child's whole outlook on religion. We must freely admit that many an inexperienced Sunday School teacher has, by the very quality of his own faith and character, been able to lead children to a profound love of our Lord and his Church. We must never lose sight of the truth that "religion is caught, not taught". But sincerity and goodwill alone—without knowledge and skill—are precarious weapons against the growing technical efficiency of trained educators; and if our Sunday Schools are to do their work effectively in our technological age they must adopt the kind of methods and techniques with which children are familiar and which command their respect. It is worth reminding ourselves that, in fact, the Sunday School movement during the last forty years has been in the forefront of educational advance; but it has taken a long time for improved methods to become at all widely adopted and there are still innumerable Sunday Schools where the instruction is flat and unimaginative and the children run riot. A bad Sunday School is worse than none at all.

Our Sunday Schools must be the best we can make them, at whatever cost. They must be, as far as possible, properly graded (so that nobody is faced with the impossible task of teaching five-year-olds side by side with older juniors or even young adolescents) and equipped with the apparatus that is the raw material of effective teaching. A glance through any handbook of modern teaching methods, whether for Sunday School or Day School, with its constant reference to pictures, charts, sand trays, flannelgraph, models, blackboard diagrams and summaries, notebooks, expression-work and mime, will reveal the extreme poverty of much of our teaching. The teachers themselves should be given every encouragement to undergo a course of training, and many dioceses (under the skilled direction of a Sunday School Adviser) now provide lectures and study courses of great value. The teacher's status within the life of the Church should be held in honour and regarded by everyone as a high vocation, to which the parish priest may make frequent reference in sermons. Teachers should be admitted to their responsible office at a public service, so that the rest of the congregation can realize that they are being commissioned on their behalf, as their representatives, and be called upon to pray for them and support them in every possible way.

By such means as this the Church's care for her children, geared to the highest possible pitch of effectiveness, can be given its true place in the life of each local congregation—the centre of interest and the focus of attention. "Jesus called a little child unto him and set him *in the midst*".

The Parish Communion

ALL that we have so far discussed of the child's training in prayer and worship comes to a focus in the Church's great central offering of worship—the Service of Holy Communion. All roads lead to that point—the consummation of all spiritual experience and the ground in which all other spiritual activity is, so to speak, rooted. It is interesting to notice how, once Baptism has reached its completion in Confirmation, the Church provides Holy Communion for every contingency of life; not only as a regular weekly (or even daily) part of the Christian warfare, but also for specific occasions of great moment: Marriage, Ordination, the moment of Death, Burial, and the Commemoration of the Departed (besides such events as the Coronation of the Sovereign or the enthronement of a Bishop)—all these are ideally performed within the setting of the Service of Holy Communion, as the Prayer Book clearly provides. The Nuptial, the Viaticum, the Requiem —it is a rich provision of spiritual blessing at every "crisis" of life and death. For this reason the child's introduction to this great central offering of the whole Church is a matter of unrivalled importance and needs a chapter to itself.

"My Communion"

Here perhaps I may be allowed to speak from personal experience. The very first time I was ever present at a Service of Holy Communion in the Church of England was on the Sunday after my Confirmation. It was also the occasion of my first Communion. I must confess that it was an anxious and disappointing experience. The service was almost completely unfamiliar to me (though I had "read it over" once or twice beforehand) and so were most of the people taking part—a small company of isolated individuals scattered at random over a wilderness of empty pews; and when it was over we all drifted away in chill silence to home and breakfast. It was a forbidding introduction for any young person to the Church's chief act of fellowship. Surely it would be hard to imagine anything less like an act of Communion or an experience of *koinonia*. About the same time someone presented me with a small devotional manual entitled "My Communion"; and both then and ever since that very title has seemed to me a contradiction in terms. If it is a "comm-union" at all—one-ness with our Lord and with each other—then it is not "*my* communion" but "*our* communion" and must surely find some satisfying expression in concrete and recognizable fellowship.

This experience throws a searching light on to what had, until recent years, become a serious weakness in the Church's dealings with her younger members, and in many quarters unhappily still is. "My Communion" emphasizes the idea of isolation, and the kind of service I have described, far from being an experience of true communion, is little more than an aggregation of separate individuals saying their own personal prayers under the same roof. Even the act of Communion itself (which does in fact, however little they may realize it, bind them into one in Christ) cannot be fully apprehended within such a setting of individualism.

Drift and Decline

We will pick up this problem at the point where we left it in the last chapter. In Baptism (as we have seen) the child is made a living member of the Family of Christ, and the

Service of Baptism stresses the truth that Confirmation and Communion are the necessary completion of this privilege. "Ye are to take care that this child be brought to the Bishop to be confirmed by him as soon as he can say the Creed, the Lord's Prayer, and the Ten Commandments in the vulgar tongue, and be further instructed in the Church Catechism set forth for that purpose." The 1928 Prayer Book very wisely draws out the implications of this charge by adding "... so that, strengthened with the gift of the Holy Spirit, he may come with due preparation to receive the Holy Communion of the Body and Blood of Christ and go forth into the world to serve God faithfully in the fellowship of his Church." These requirements, as we saw, do not assume a very advanced stage of instruction, and it was clearly the mind of those who compiled the Book of Common Prayer that children should, as a matter of course and as early as possible, be brought to Confirmation and Communion. That is the whole purport of the vows undertaken by parents and godparents at the font. Yet, as we know, thousands of the babies baptized every Sunday at our fonts are never brought to be instructed in the Faith. Of those who are, a high proportion come only to a Sunday School, which all too often may have only the most tenuous link with the worshipping congregation, and may sometimes indeed be in direct competition with it. Many will be sent to the Sunday School of some other denomination, because the parents are left to imagine that any kind of religious teaching will do, and no one has ever told them that this is a serious infringement of the vows of sponsorship. In many other instances children may come to Matins or Evensong for years, and even reach the stage of Confirmation, without even once being present at the Service of Holy Communion, which is the one great focal point of their membership in the Body of Christ. It is a confused and disheartening picture, and it ought not to surprise us that so many fall by the way, and that others who do reach Confirmation scarcely survive their first experience of Communion. The responsibility for this sad state of things rests four-square on the Church itself. We lament the steady drainage of children from the life of the Church. The figures are appalling. Out of every hundred babies baptized only forty ever reach the stage of Confirmation. (Actually more than fifty per cent are never even sent to the Church for teaching.) Of these forty who are eventually confirmed, so many lapse that only ten of them make even their Easter Communion; and, as we know only too well, the figures for Easter Communions are a false indication of the true communicant strength of the Church. Out of that original hundred only two or three become regular communicants. It is a desperate situation, and the remedy lies only in our own hands. Until the Church as a whole becomes really concerned and conscience-stricken about this unhappy state of things the process of drift will continue and the young life will drain away in a steady decline.

1927 ff.

During the last thirty years the Liturgical Movement (with its stress on the Parish Communion) has been attempting to deal realistically with this situation by restoring the Service of Holy Communion to its obviously central place in the worship of the Church; and this is a thing that has enormous importance also as an educational instrument in the Church's dealing with her children. It is proving successful because it is founded on sound principles of worship. No one who examines impartially the formularies of the Church of England can honestly doubt that the Holy Communion is there intended to be the most important act of the Christian Community. It is the Lord's own service, expressly instituted and commanded; the one observance held and honoured in common by all Christians, except the Quakers (who in any case have their own "spiritual" counterpart of it). The Book of Common Prayer, following the age-long tradition of Christendom, explicitly intends that the Holy Communion should be the chief and central service of every Sunday and Holy day. It provides a Collect, Epistle, and Gospel for every Sunday of the year, as well as for the Red Letter days of obligation. The rubrics after the Nicene Creed are the only place in the Prayer Book where the priest is enjoined to give out notices and banns and to preach a sermon. It is clearly meant to be the one service at which everybody, as far as possible, is expected to be present. The rubrics at the end of the service make it plain that it is also intended to be a service at which as many people as possible should receive Communion. All this underlines very emphatically the Church's insistence on the Holy Communion as her most important offering of worship and one with which children ought to be made familiar from their earliest years. If strict obedience to the Prayer Book is to be taken seriously, here is a simple standard that can be very readily applied. Since we are in fact losing our grip every year on thousands of children who come under our pastoral care, perhaps a return, in simple obedience, to the age-old wisdom of the Church may yet prove to be the remedy. Where this is actually being done the results are remarkable enough to deserve our most careful examination.

c. *A New Approach*

In contrast with my own disappointing experience of a first Communion (and it is an experience which many young people are still having to undergo) let me paint another picture, from later and more fortunate experience, of how we may give our children a happier approach to the altar of God, helping them to grow naturally and imperceptibly to their full stature as members of the Body of Christ, from Baptism onwards. The essential core of this approach is some form of Parish Communion at which the whole congregation, young and old, can reasonably be expected to be present.

It begins with the child's Baptism; and here, as we instruct parents and godparents about the meaning of their vows, we must with all love and sympathy insist firmly on the fact that what begins in Baptism cannot be properly completed and fulfilled until the child has been confirmed and become a regular communicant. No one should ever be allowed to undertake these solemn commitments without realizing the thoroughly practical implications of them, and we must help sponsors—and above all parents—to see these promises as a direct challenge to their own personal integrity, and to realize the solemn truth that to ignore or flout these promises is a sin. They will be answerable to God for the child's eternal welfare. It is an almost frightening responsibility. When this is explained with sympathy and urgency, many parents and sponsors, for the sake of the children as well as on their own account, can be prevailed upon to seek Confirmation themselves, or to make a new start if they have lapsed. But in any case (as we have already seen in several other connections) it is most important that we should provide them with the kind of setting within which they can be expected to carry out their promises with some hope of succeeding. To come to church themselves and to bring their children with them—that is obviously the ideal. But have we the kind of services to offer them at which this would be either practicable or desirable? That is the crux of the whole problem—and some form of Parish Communion may be the very answer we are looking for.

At the time of the child's Baptism and in the instruction surrounding it, we shall be wise to suggest to the parents some of those simple ways we discussed in a previous chapter (pages 106ff) in which the child as he grows up can be made familiar with the inside of the church and come to feel at home in it; and this teaching will be all the more profitable if we can, at the same time, offer them the right kind of family Communion to which they can bring the child regularly from his babyhood. Let me here describe the kind of service which is fast becoming customary in many churches of all persuasions, both Evangelical and Catholic, so that we may examine its value as an educational instrument. (For we must recognize the truth that all communal acts of worship are inevitably a medium of teaching, because they are all the time communicating ideas and presuppositions to those taking part, and we can never be indifferent to the impact that a service makes on the worshippers however much we may wish to regard it as directed purely towards God.)[1]

℗ *A typical Parish Communion*

It is a simple Sung Eucharist, at a conveniently early hour (9 or 9.30 a.m.), with hymns and a brief address, as the chief service on Sunday morning, at which most members of the church will be encouraged to be present and, if possible, make their communion. Parents are invited to come with their children, even tiny babies, and sit together as a family. Older children will generally prefer to sit with their friends, but that need never destroy the family atmosphere. Such a service can be a Family Service in two senses: a service in which whole families come and worship together, and a service which expresses the Family spirit of the whole congregation. This is also, *par excellence*, the service to which the children of non-Christian families may be invited to come under the care and friendly oversight of members of the church who may have no particular vocation for other kinds of work with children. When the parents and older people come up to make their communion they are invited to bring the little ones with them to the altar

[1] See below (pp. 151ff).

<u>rail</u>. The toddlers can kneel side by side with them, and there is no reason why a mother should not receive communion with a baby in her arms. <u>As the priest gives communion, he pauses for a moment to bless the babies and children</u>, resting his hand for a moment on their heads as he says a simple "God bless you and keep you always".

Such a service is not only an exhilarating experience of "family" worship at its highest; it is also an impressive means of helping children to find their place naturally in the worshipping life of the Church and of helping adult members of the congregation to recognize their responsibility for every child baptized at the parish font. As children grow in that setting they will never be able to look back on a time in their life when they were not familiar with the Church's chief act of worship. Week by week they will see the altar thronged with communicants; they will have their own simple share in the great moment of Communion, and they will come to long for the time when they too may receive the sacred bread and wine. One little boy of four asked "When can I have a drink too, like Daddy?" which is only another way of asking, "What mean ye by this service?" The words and acts of the service are printed indelibly on their minds and they grow by imperceptible degrees to the stage where Confirmation is the inevitable and desirable next step.

E *A Teaching Aid*

This kind of approach is another example of that educational principle we have continually stressed—inducing the child's growth in worship by <u>appealing to his overriding desire to be grown-up and by allowing him to share in an adult act</u>. It is for this reason that I suggested in the previous chapter that <u>it is in general an educational mistake to isolate children from the corporate worship of the whole congregation and a psychological error to lay undue stress</u>

on their immaturity. We have several times noted the danger that they may all too readily come to associate religion with childhood and immaturity. But naturally this will not mean ignoring their immaturity altogether. That would be equally disastrous. One great educational value of the Eucharist is that it is teaching all the time by its very action. It is a *drama*, and it is all the more fascinating to young children because it provides so many things to watch and do. This is the obvious advantage of the Eucharist over the more "intellectual" kinds of service, which demand a degree of mental concentration of which children (as well as many adults) are not capable. The actual instruction at the Eucharist may have the children specially in mind and will be all the better for being simple, pictorial, and brief—and, above all things, an integral part of the worship. This kind of instruction is also more acceptable to most adults, as our Lord recognized in his constant use of parables. It can be a short exposition of Collect, Epistle, or Gospel, or an explanation of some part of the action. The whole of religion is concentrated in the action of the Eucharist, and it is the perfect instrument of instruction in the faith.

F. Practical Advantages

This kind of Parish Communion also helps, incidentally, to solve many practical problems. How many mothers there must be who could never be expected to make their communion unless they could bring their young children to church with them; and even then they are often reluctant to leave them behind in the pews while they come up to the altar. How many children there are in our Sunday Schools who never come to church and to whom Communion is, at the best, remote hearsay, and likely to remain so. Weekly worship at the altar may well be made a matter of simple obligation for all who claim membership of the parish organizations; and if there had to be a choice between Sunday School or the Eucharist, the Eucharist should come first. As we have seen, the Sunday School is not fulfilling its purpose unless it is leading children to the altar. Where such a rule of worship at the Eucharist is made a matter of moral obligation (as indeed it should always be) the Service of Holy Communion can be made the basis of all instruction for Confirmation. The Bishop of Warrington has produced an admirable series of Confirmation talks, based entirely on the movement of the Eucharist.[1] Where something of this kind is used, Confirmation candidates can then be required to begin as we expect them to continue, by being regularly present at the Eucharist every Sunday during their preparation—a rule we cannot possibly insist on if the only celebration is at an early hour with only a handful of occasional communicants, but quite simple if the Eucharist is the chief service of Sunday morning with the whole "Family" present. The Confirmation instructions can then be a fascinating explanation and commentary on things with which they are already becoming familiar in practice; and when the time comes for their first Communion it will happen within a setting which is already a regular part of their life, with no embarrassment or anxiety.

G. *A Reassurance.*

Many people are shy of this kind of service because they fear that the presence of young children at the Eucharist will destroy the atmosphere of quiet reverence which many older people have come (sometimes rather selfishly) to value. But experience does not bear this out. It is true that it will be much more of a homely, family occasion, which is all to the good; but children quickly catch the atmosphere of quiet reverence from older people, and where a true spirit

[1] These are available from The Children's Council, 69, Great Peter Street, London, S.W.1.

of worship is prevailing we need never fear to bring children in. Special provision may sometimes have to be made for tiny ones who are more than usually vociferous; but where there is sympathy and goodwill this need never be an undue difficulty. In such problems the family spirit finds quite spontaneous expression, and some young member of the congregation will be found ready to take the baby into the porch for a few minutes while the mother makes her Communion. Where a too large number of young children creates a problem, some of the Young Wives or a group of girls from the Youth Club might organize a crèche in the parish hall for the more restless ones, or as a refuge for any who get tired before the service is over. But I suggest that the crèche should be regarded only as a second line of defence! The desirable thing is that the children should be at the service, and in my own experience (though of course there are bound to be lapses from time to time) children will take a fascinated part and behave admirably as long as real and reverent worship is being offered by older people.

This has been a mere sketch of what is in fact proving a most powerful means of drawing and winning the children of the Church—and their parents. The value of it is that, besides being in harmony with the age-long practice of Christendom, it is rooted in sound educational principles. It will need adapting to the varying needs of parishes, but the guiding principles remain inviolate. In the rapidly changing conditions of the present time this is likely to prove more and more to be the most effective way of grafting our younger members securely into the Body of Christ's Church.

Two books on the Parish Communion for further study:

The Parish Communion, edited by A. G. Hebert, S.S.M. (S.P.C.K.).
Sunday Morning: the New Way, edited by Brother Edward (S.P.C.K.).

11

Worship in the Day School

THE Church—the Divine Society and worshipping community—is absolutely central in the Christian Religion. There can be no true discipleship outside and apart from the Body of Christ, and much of our discussion about problems of prayer and worship and the Christian way of life tends to be confused and inconclusive because we too readily equate the *anima naturaliter Christiana* (the Christian temper of mind, unrelated to Christian theology and devotion) with the Christian Religion. The "Christian spirit" is not in itself enough. It may indeed survive, as a kind of afterglow, in a generation that has long since abandoned Christian belief and practice. That has been described as "living on our Christian capital". To draw an analogy from *Alice in Wonderland*, it is like the grin that remained behind when the Chesire Cat had vanished; but once the Cat has gone it cannot be long before the grin disappears too, because the grin is (so to speak) an attribute of the Cat and cannot exist without it! This explains why, in our survey of the whole field of prayer and worship, we have been so much concerned with the task of integrating the growing child into the worshipping life of the Church.

A. PRINCIPLES OF SCHOOL WORSHIP

It is important to keep this fundamental truth clearly in view as we come to consider the question of worship in the day school. It will be helpful to recall here certain clear principles which we laid down at the beginning, because they will be our guide through many of the difficulties which are peculiar to school worship. We saw how worship is "the all-pervading recognition of the absolute worth of God". Because this is God's universe, nothing in it can be properly understood except in the light of God's creative purpose, which is paramount and all-pervasive. This means seeing everything (even the most trivial details of daily life) *sub specie aeternitatis,* in the light of eternity. We can only rightly judge and value the *means* by the *end* to which they are directed. The material world, which is temporal and contingent, can be safely handled and directed only when we see it all the time as a medium through which God is working out a plan which is to reach its fulfilment beyond death, in the eternal world. Once we see the whole of life within that setting of eternity we see it in its true perspective. Worship, therefore, is acknowledging, both in theory and practice, the absolute supremacy of God throughout the whole natural order—and that is the only true estimate of his "worth".

We saw too how such "worship" must engage the whole personality and permeate the whole field of living. I acknowledge God's pre-eminence not only with my intellect, but also with my affections and my will. So worship is far more than a purely verbal expression of homage or an intellectual acceptance of theological ideas. I honour God and acknowledge his supremacy by the sort of person I am and the standards I live by. The core of worship is the conformity of belief with practice (which incidentally is the first tenet of Marxism!). As we train children in worship it is most important to preserve this balance. But, as we have seen, none of this begins to be possible outside the provision which God has made within the sacramental life of his Church; and it is within this majestic context of Christian worship that the problems peculiar to the Day School must always be approached.

B *Limitations of School Worship*

The chief difficulty about school worship is that, in all except Church schools, it is quite unavoidably the "worship of our lips" largely divorced from the life of the Christian community. Any acts of worship which are not an integral part of the offering of the Body of Christ are only of the nature of "private devotions", with all the accompanying dangers of individualism. So one of our chief problems is somehow to relate school worship to the worship of the). Church and the whole practice of the Christian Religion.

In Aided Church schools this can be done by the closest possible association with the parish church. In other schools (including Controlled Church schools) it is only possible to point to the Church, in an objective way, as the divine Society which in her liturgy offers to God the only true corporate worship "in Christ" and of which we all need to be ourselves worshipping members. But it is important that this should be done—and done clearly and emphatically—so that the school assembly may never be allowed to appear as a substitute for the worship of the Church. This warning is most necessary when one considers the growing number of day schools that provide (sometimes on Sundays) services which are expressly intended to take the place of Church worship and are thereby usurping a function that can never belong to them. The justification is often given that the children who attend these services would not in any case attend a church. That plea has a great deal of force, and where they are deliberately used as a preparation for the Gospel, pointing all the time beyond themselves to the Church of Christ as an essential part of the Gospel, they may indeed serve a most valuable purpose in evangelism. But where the means becomes an end in itself the results can only be confusing and disastrous in the long run. Even if the children are never persuaded to "join" the

Church at some point, by becoming members of some particular denomination, at least they must never be left in doubt that it is impossible to be a true and complete Christian without doing so.

For thousands of children in our schools, the School Assembly will be their one contact with the Christian Faith and their only opportunity of learning what personal prayer and corporate worship really mean. That is why it is so desperately urgent that what they learn from these acts should be the whole Christian truth and not a garbled version of it. The challenge must always be there, whatever their response may be; and it is only when the challenge is perfectly clear that there is any hope of a positive response. That is why in school worship the claims of the Church must always be kept clearly in sight. I must add that, in the present divided state of Christendom, we are bound to mean, when we talk about joining the Church at some point, a definite denominational allegiance. The best Agreed Syllabuses emphasize this truth.

So the school assembly can be only a "preparation for the Gospel"—a means of introducing Christian truth and practice to many who would otherwise remain untouched by it. But it is an immensely powerful means—far more effective and compelling than any form of direct instruction. That is a fact that we need to ponder very carefully as we go on now to consider ways of using to the best advantage the opportunities now offered in the day schools of conducting acts of Christian worship.

c. The School Assembly

The Education Act of 1944 made it a matter of statutory obligation throughout the country, and not merely of local option, that every school, whether a church or a county school, must begin the day with a collective act of worship. In the two kinds of Church of England schools, whether

Aided or Controlled, this act of worship can and ought to be fully Anglican. In the Aided School, which preserves without compromise all the old privileges of the Church School, it is only to be expected that the worship will be Church worship at its fullest, with a generous use of the Prayer Book and frequent services in the Parish Church, including the Eucharist. In the Controlled School too, the opening act of worship may be in accordance with the original trust deed of the school—and that means that it can preserve definite Anglican characteristics. This is a matter of extreme importance. It brings us back to the point we made above —that an act of worship is a more powerful means of teaching the Faith than any form of deliberate instruction.

In case this sounds like a wrong motive—to regard an act of worship as a means of teaching—let me hasten to say that, whatever our feelings about it may be, any act of worship, good or bad, Christian, pagan, or synthetic, is inevitably teaching a "faith"; it is instilling, generally quite unconsciously, into the minds of those taking part, certain ideas about the nature of God and of our approach to him in prayer. The presuppositions, theological and devotional, on which any act of worship is based (even where they are never explicitly stated) penetrate deeply into the mind of the worshipper and shape for good or ill his whole conception of religion. We must look at this truth in some detail.

The very act of praying at all assumes, without argument, certain truths about God. It assumes, to begin with, that God exists; it also assumes that he is in close touch with us, able to hear our petitions, and in a position to do something about them. So the very simplest beginning of prayer, "O God...", assumes a whole body of implicit theological truth. If I go further and say, "Almighty God...", or further still and say "Almighty Father, who hast given thine only son to die for our sins and rise again

for our justification . . .", then the implicit theological truth
is obviously becoming more and more pronounced. In fact,
I cannot say the two words "Our Father . . ." or finish a
prayer with the formula "through Jesus Christ our Lord",
without finding myself confronted by dogmatic assertions
about God and the world at large which an atheist or an
agnostic is perfectly free to dispute. Prayer is saturated with
theology.

Worship imparts Belief

This illustrates a most important characteristic of worship—that any act of worship, from the simplest grace
before meals to the most elaborate liturgical rite, is an
implicit confession of faith. *Lex orandi, lex credendi.* The
very words which we use to address God also describe God's
attributes; and it is because in worship these attributes of
God are simply taken for granted, and not argued or
deliberately taught, that worship is the most powerful
medium of all for communicating dogmatic truth. It is
far more powerful than the direct instruction of the classroom, simply because it teaches incidentally and by implica-
tion; and it is the things that are taken for granted, the
implicit assumptions, rather than any kind of explicit
teaching, that sink most deeply into the subconscious mind
and become the foundations of "faith". For this reason (if
for no other) we need to take the greatest possible care
with the choice of material in our worship. It is all the
time teaching at a deeper and more enduring level than
the "Scripture lesson" can ever hope to do. Call this "indoctrination" if you like, but some degree of indoctrination
is inevitable in all effective education.[1]

[1] Some quotations from Professor M. V. C. Jeffreys' book
Glaucon bear on this point. "No true education can escape the
responsibility of communicating a *view of life*—that is, of 'indoc-
trinating'." . . . "The cult of the open mind is a way of camou-

False theology in the classroom is regrettable, but not always very serious. Children will question false theology as well as true. But false theology in worship (where it is unquestioned) is disastrous; because it is through the un-argued assumptions of hymns and prayers (not to mention stained glass windows, illustrated manuals of devotion, and the general attitude of grown-up people) that children grow in their knowledge of God and the practice of religion. When we remind ourselves again that, for most children in our schools, the morning assembly is their only formal contact with God and their only training in prayer (com peting on unequal terms with all the other influences on their lives in which the basic assumptions are godless) it is clearly urgent that the worship to which we accustom them should be thoroughly sound, both theologically and devotionally.

Theological Truth

Perhaps this can be best illustrated by looking at certain ways in which school worship may be deficient in these two aspects—*theology* and *devotion*. There are many books provided for use in school assemblies in which the conception of worship is inadequate and sometimes even heretical. On the theological side, the most common weakness, specially with juniors, is an undue stress on the beauties of Nature, bordering on pantheism, often with little reference to God at all. The great acts of God in the Incarnation, the Cross, the Resurrection, the Ascension, Pentecost, and the life of the Christian Church, are barely touched upon, if at all. In

flaging the poverty of an education which has no view of life to communicate. *Indoctrination is not an educational crime, but an educational necessity.*" (Italics mine.) "The crime is to indoctrinate in such a way as to destroy the freedom and responsibility of the pupil." Our business is to "present a strongly held faith in such a way as to challenge the beholder to come to terms with it on his own personal responsibility." (M. V. C. Jeffreys, *Glaucon*, Pitmans.)

some books provided for junior worship "unpleasant" things (such as illness, pain, wrongdoing—together with the Cross and all references to death and the after life) are deliberately excluded, on the express grounds that for young children religion should be a "joyous" thing; but can it ever be a "joyous" thing in any true sense if it leaves unanswered all the most urgent questions that children are capable of asking at a very early age? It will merely misrepresent religion as a spurious delight in natural beauty and so distort the child's growing idea of God. So we should carefully avoid any hymns or prayers which gloss over the great dogmas of the faith in favour of pantheistic nature-worship, Pelagian self-sufficiency, or ("These things shall be .. !") unblushing scientific humanism.

The very materials of which any act of worship is composed—prayers, hymns, readings, and so on—will be all the time conveying to the worshippers religious ideas, for good or ill. The fatal thing is when any of these ingredients are so defective that they confront the worshipper with half-truths or even positive falsities. The glory of the ancient liturgy of the Church is that it presents us with the full truth, stated in beautiful and measured language, free from all heretical bias or passing fashions of sentiment, progressively revealed through the drama of the Church's year. By contrast, so many modern efforts at liturgy and service-building are theologically defective and sometimes even heretical. Many are sentimental, fulsome, and sententious, and couched in execrable English! In that case they cannot avoid presenting the worshipper with false images of God. Some of the hymns, for example, which children are invited to sing are only thinly disguised nature-worship or self-assured humanism. There is plenty of room in worship for the hymn of rejoicing and *joie de vivre*, but it must be centred on God and never be at the expense of overlooking, or even worse denying, man's sinfulness and need of God's grace. Some modern hymn books have done a serious dis-service in this respect, editing great Christian hymns in such a way that they can be sung without offence by prac-tically anybody, quite regardless of their religious beliefs. Beware of what someone has aptly called "gallant and high-handed heartiness"! This kind of devotion divorced from theology can only convey damaging untruths to children who drink it in.

Devotional Truth

Besides theological soundness worship must also have devotional balance. Remember again that for most of the children in our schools, the School Assembly will be their one experience of prayer and the only instruction they will ever receive in worship. They will learn by doing—im-plicitly. So we must be careful to let them experience the whole range of worship—Adoration, Confession, Thanks-giving, Supplication (in its two forms, Petition for our-selves and Intercession for others), and Self-oblation. Here again there is a danger, specially with junior worship, of concentrating largely on Thanksgiving—with perhaps limited forms of Supplication—and omitting altogether the more profound acts of adoration (in which children delight), simple acts of penitence for wrong-doing, and prayers of self-offering and the dedication of work. Naturally it will be impossible, in every individual act of school worship, to cover the whole field of devotion; but we must see that the balance is preserved at least during the course of a whole week, devoting one morning to Adoration (with other acts subordinate), another to Confession, and so on. In that way we can make sure that the children will at least become familiar with prayer in all its forms. It adds enormously to the power of this implicit teaching if you assume (and occasionally say so) that the children might like to use this hymn or that prayer when they say their own private prayers night and morning. That will impress upon them, without direct instruction, the idea that prayer is a normal part of daily life.

Theological truth and *devotional integrity* are largely (though not entirely) a matter of using good books. From this standpoint perhaps the two best books are the *Oxford Book of School Worship* and *School Worship Day by Day*, both published by S.P.C.K.[1] Within the sound framework that these books provide (which includes among other things valuable guidance about the choice of hymns and lessons), material from other sources can be added at will.

So there is the twofold influence of school worship in imparting theology and devotion. It compels us to look closely at the acts of worship we devise and conduct and ask ourselves the searching question: "Is this showing my children the full truth about God—and is it introducing them to the full practice of prayer?" Because here, in our hands, is a tremendous force that cannot be neutral. It will *teach*, and teach powerfully, whether we like it or not. We must do everything we can to see that what it teaches is the whole Christian truth, both theological and devotional, and nothing less.

Before we go on to consider further the choice of suitable material and the actual conduct of worship, there are two other important considerations which bear upon the nature of worship and go deep to the roots of all its practical problems.

The Sense of Awe

The first is that an act of worship must always provoke in the worshipper a sense of the wonder and mystery of God. Worship is (as Evelyn Underhill has expressed it) "an acknowledgement of transcendence".[2] Children very readily

[1] For further Bibliography, see Note 2 on page 172.
[2] For the full quotation, see page 18.

appreciate the kind of hymns and prayers which express this sense of "numinous awe", and we should be careful never to allow our school worship to degenerate into a hearty and materialistic preoccupation with ourselves and the physical world.

But at the same time (because God is immanent as well as transcendent) worship must also be closely related to all experience and all knowledge. Not only must we help children to understand the need for conformity between worship and life (and the whole ethos of a school is the most powerful means of subconsciously conveying this truth) but our worship must also come to terms with so-called "secular" knowledge, so that there is no longer a disastrous dichotomy between what we learn in the Science or Biology period and what we say or sing in the School Assembly. True Christian worship can achieve (and it is the only thing in the world that can) what the Germans call a *Weltanschauung*—an integrated and coherent view of the whole universe and every branch of knowledge, with the supremacy of God (both in knowledge and experience) as the clue to the whole puzzle. That is why the Church school will always remain the most effective means of Christian education.[1]

THE CHOICE OF MATERIAL

So our chief concern, in choosing material for the school assembly (hymns, reading, prayers, and so on) is to ensure that they are the kind of material that can communicate to the worshippers implicit theological and devotional truth; that is, knowledge of God and experience of prayer. But the choice of suitable material involves two other consider-ations. There is first the much-debated question of what children are, or are not, capable of understanding (and with this is bound up the whole problem of interest); and

[1] See Note 1 (*The Divided Curriculum*) on page 170.

secondly there is the question of how to provide for the greatest amount of active co-operation (which in itself comprises more than half of the problem of interest).

Understanding

Look first at the question of "understanding". Many people feel that children should never be allowed to join in hymns or prayers which are "beyond their understanding". But it is not easy to define what is beyond their understanding. Worship has so much in common with the arts (especially poetry) that I cannot forbear to quote again that illuminating remark of T. S. Eliot: "Genuine poetry can communicate before it is understood." That is true of the great hymns and prayers of the Church. Children feel and appreciate the sense of wonder, awe, gratitude, or self-abasement, expressed in majestic words, long before they are able to grasp the meaning of the words themselves. This is quite different from saying that—

> *The meaning doesn't matter*
> *If it's only idle chatter*
> *Of a transcendental kind!*

The meaning does matter; what doesn't matter is whether children can fully grasp it intellectually. The meaning (as long as it is there) may be sensed at a profound spiritual level before it is understood with the mind. So if we want our children to have the deepest experience of worship we shall be wise not to limit them to the simple (sometimes almost inane) prayers and hymns that we think they will "understand". We shall avoid the kind of hymns and prayers specially written for children which talk to God as if he were a half-witted governess! They are very common. It is true that with infants the choice of hymns and prayers must be determined by the limitations of their vocabulary and their difficulty in pronouncing any but the simplest words. Fortunately there is plenty of splendid material provided for them—hymns like "Jesus' hands are kind hands", "Two little eyes to look to God", "Praise him, praise him, all you little children", "Thank you for the world so sweet", and so on. But any time after the age of five let children begin to learn and use the finest adult hymns and prayers of our Christian heritage. Between five and seven we shall probably be wise to limit the selection to the narrative type of hymn—the hymn that tells a story or paints a picture or has an attractive refrain. All the Christmas and Easter hymns are of this character, together with such favourites as "Advent tells us Christ is near", "On Jordan's bank", "There is a green hill", "Loving Shepherd", "Hail the day that sees him rise", "Jesus, good above all other", "All creatures of our God and King", "I was made a Christian". That rather random selection illustrates the kind of hymns quite suitable for children from five to seven.

But after the age of seven there is no reason why they should not begin to sing fully adult hymns. Naturally we shall avoid hymns which express emotions or aspirations completely outside their experience, that is, strongly subjective hymns (which have obvious dangers even for adults); but the great objective statements of fact or faith (such as "Praise to the Holiest" or "Immortal, invisible", or "St Patrick's Breastplate") are perfectly within the compass of quite young children. Give them the chance to use them and they will soon let you know whether they prefer such hymns to "We are but little children weak" (which no normal child could possibly sing with honest conviction!).

Readings

The same principle will govern the choice of readings. We may be tempted, specially in junior worship, to confine the readings to what are regarded, I think erroneously, as "simple Gospel stories". (In fact no Gospel stories are really simple; the problems they raise at every point are always tremendous and profound.) Let the children hear occasionally some of the great resounding passages from the Prophets or the Epistles, read as impressively as possible (preferably by an adult who knows how to read) within the setting of a "theme" service which can help to elucidate their meaning. This is not setting a premium on the unintelligible! That would be foolish. I am only pleading that we should not allow our choice to be restricted by a false conception of what children can easily comprehend. There are some books of school worship which, in their search for suitable readings, will range widely over the whole field of literature (sacred and profane)—with selections from Keats or the Koran—in the effort to provide something palatable and intelligible! Such readings may indeed have great value if, within the setting of a Christian act of worship, they can be used to illuminate some aspect of Christian truth; but far too often they may be nothing more than a semi-pagan or merely aesthetic experience. The word of God must always be our chief source of devotional readings, and if we will give our children opportunities of listening to God's word, the Holy Spirit will be able to speak to them in his own way at their own level.

The question of interest is also involved here. It is, I suggest, a mistake to suppose that with children interest is always a matter of comprehension. A sense of "numinous awe", of the *mysterium tremendum*, in an act of prostrate adoration, will often be far more "interesting" and satisfying to a child than the mere meaning of some shallow and obvious sentiment played down to his supposed level of understanding. But I am not suggesting for a moment that we should ever underrate the element of understanding, and there will often be occasions when we may wish to substitute for an ordinary Bible reading either a modern version (such as the one by Monsignor Knox) or a well-written passage from Christian biography or devotional writing. It is worth noting, in passing, that probably the best version of the Bible for use in worship is the American Revised Standard Version, because it keeps very closely to the original quality of the Authorized Version (with which we shall wish to familiarize the children), while making the more obscure passages crystal clear.

Co-operation

The second consideration that will govern our choice of material is *co-operation*. For a child (as for an adult) a good deal of the interest he will find in a service depends on the share he is allowed to take in it. It is a pity that his part should be limited (as it so often is) to hymns and Amens. We may encourage the children to follow the reading in their own Bibles, as well as to observe a short period of silent reflection (perhaps fifteen seconds or so) after it. This is a surer incentive to real co-operation even than having children as lectors. But it is the prayers which afford the most satisfying opportunities for shared activity at a deep level. There are many interesting varieties of prayer-forms (all illustrated in such a book as the *Oxford Book of School Worship*). You may suggest subjects of prayer in a few simple biddings, leaving the children free to pray for a few moments in silence and then summarizing their prayers either by a versicle and response or with a brief collect. Several short, succinct prayers, each on a definite point, are always better than one long one containing several ideas. Again, you may use a simple litany—and the most suitable type of litany for children is one in which short *preces* and *responses* follow each other in rapid succession. From time to time you will want to use some of the great classical prayers of Christendom—often enough for children to learn them by frequent repetition and to join in them spontaneously. It is an important part of their training in worship that they should be helped to stock their minds with great words hallowed by centuries of use.

Be careful, in acts of Confession, Thanksgiving, or Petition, always to start from some point in the children's own experience, passing from the particular to the general. Instead of saying such things as "Let us pray for all men everywhere" (an impossible kind of prayer that makes no appeal to the imagination!), you can say "Let us pray for Tom Smith who is ill—and we will make this a prayer for *all* people who are ill." Above all, do everything possible to redeem the Lord's Prayer from familiar over-usage. Vary the use of it—sometimes repeated phrase by phrase, with silent pauses; sometimes said with a special "intention" (remembering that the "Our Father" can be used in itself as a specific act of Adoration, Confession, Thanksgiving, or Supplication, with any particular slant we like to give it); sometimes sung to a good setting; sometimes said silently. It happens so often, in the school assembly, that the Lord's Prayer is the one point where the service is most liable to lapse into a barren formality and even irreverence. Use it sparingly and with careful preparation so that it may be the perfect summary of all prayers.

Themes and the Church's Year

There is one other important consideration governing the choice of material and linked with the problem of interest. Let school worship always be closely related to the Church's year. The Church in her wisdom has provided us with a series of fascinating "themes", beginning during the first half of the year, at Advent and Christmas, with our Lord's early life, and leading steadily through the historic events of his Ministry to the Ascension and Whitsuntide. In the second half of the year (during Trinity-tide) we are invited to ponder on the meaning of our faith and its application to everyday life. It is wise to adhere closely to that scheme.

There is no merit in singing Easter hymns during Lent, or Good Friday hymns at Whitsun, as happens quite frequently! Owing to the timing of holidays there may be a strong argument for forestalling both Christmas and Easter in school worship so that children who do not go to church may not altogether miss the devotional celebration of these great events; but, if it does prove desirable to sing of the triumph of Easter before the events of Holy Week, make it quite clear to the children that you are in fact anticipating the Feast itself, and urge them to observe Holy Week and specially Good Friday so that they may be able to understand the triumphant joy of Easter worship. Christmas and Easter may sometimes need that exceptional handling in schools; but for the rest of the year it is best to stick to the calendar. *School Worship Day by Day*, by R. C. Arundale (S.P.C.K.) provides material under suitable themes to cover the whole of the Church's year.

LEADING SCHOOL WORSHIP

The School Assembly is not just an opening ceremony, a mere formality, a kind of spiritual "kick-off" for the day, otherwise unrelated to the affairs of the school. It should be a most realistic preparation for the day's activities, setting the tone (so to speak) of all that follows, closely integrated with the whole of school life. All the most vital concerns and interests of the school—from examinations and house matches to the work of the classrooms or the illness of a pupil—should find their place in the morning assembly. It is there that the *ethos* of the school should have its chief source of inspiration. It should be nothing less than the whole school dedicating itself to God.

Therefore let it always begin with God—never with ourselves and our own needs. This is an important principle of all worship, whether personal or corporate. It must begin by focusing our thoughts on God, remembering his presence, recalling his love and concern, adoring him for his goodness and power; and only within that setting of recollection shall we go on to offer other kinds of prayer concerning our own penitence, thankfulness, or requests. It is in the Lord's Prayer that we see the perfect pattern of all worship, beginning with God and his glory and passing on to contemplate the needs of the world in the light of God's purpose.

A school assembly should be composed of at least the following items: a quiet Act of Recollection, including a short prayer of preparation for worship; a hymn; a short reading (or talk); and two or three brief prayers. That seems to me the smallest framework within which anything worthwhile can be fitted; but, where nothing more is possible, even such a brief daily act, over a period of time, will afford opportunities for offering prayer in all its different forms. Anything less than that would, with children, probably be too cursory and unimpressive to make very much impact. But to this minimum framework can be added other items—a psalm or canticle, another hymn, more extensive prayers, and perhaps a piece of music (on piano or radiogram) to which the children can listen as an integral part of the service. The B.B.C. Broadcast Service for Schools every Tuesday and Friday morning demonstrates how a service of this kind can be devised, with great variety, within a regular pattern.

Conducting Worship

The art of conducting an act of worship follows the same general principles, whether in church, school, or club. Most of them are comprised under the two headings, *Reverence* and *Interest*. It is worth remembering that any act of corporate worship requires the same care in production, the same discipline of voice and demeanour, and the same careful balance and order, as the production of a play; otherwise it is liable to become dull, disorderly, and slipshod.

Reverence

Reverence comprises first of all the whole question of personal demeanour, both in the leader and in those taking part. It is quite imperative that the leader should conduct himself with composure and dignity; and that he should be more concerned to say his own prayers and offer his own worship than to see that the children are doing so. This is another instance of where the spirit of devotion is imparted by contagion and not by instruction. This will have its due effect on the leader's whole bearing, the tone of his voice, the care of enunciation, the restraint of gesture, and so on. To begin an act of worship in a very quiet voice, barely audible at the back of the hall, will do more to produce an atmosphere of expectant reverence than any more deliberate means. The demeanour of the staff during the school assembly is also an important factor in promoting or destroying an atmosphere of reverence. The moods—as well as the prejudices—of adults communicate themselves to children by a kind of contagion; and any member of the staff who exhibits scorn, indifference, or frank boredom (especially if he is a popular teacher) will have a most destructive influence on the children's appraisal of worship. This is a matter which must be laid on the conscience of the whole staff, and any who are not willing to accept the personal disciplines which the worship of God lays upon them should be invited to absent themselves; because refusing to take part in an activity that you disapprove of or despise is a more honest thing and commands greater respect from children than a participation which is patently insincere.

The Use of Silence

An atmosphere of reverence may be induced by a careful use of silence, whether or not we make use of preliminary music. If we do use music it is good to have a short, self-contained theme (lasting not more than a minute or so) to which the children can be invited to listen as they compose their thoughts in God's presence. In other words it should be a carefully integrated part of the actual service and not merely a prelude to cover the shuffling and conversation of the children's entry.[1] Always begin any act of worship with a brief "guided" silence ("Our Lord Jesus Christ is with us. . . . Let us think of him for a few moments in silence"), followed by a prayer of worship or preparation, such as the Collect for Purity. This use of silence is not only devotional; it is also disciplinary. It is far more effective than sharp and noisy commands or thumping on a bell, which can only shatter any atmosphere of expectant quietness. Use silence too, at other strategic parts of the service—after the Reading (where silence gives an opportunity for great words to sink deeply into the mind); after biddings suggesting private acts of prayer; after the blessing at the end. But remember that, if they are to use such silences effectively, the children must be ready for them and know beforehand how they are expected to use them. There is nothing more disconcerting than to find yourself suddenly suspended, so to speak, in a void of unexpected silence, wondering what is to happen next! Say quite clearly: "During the silence after the reading we will think about these words of our Lord and try to understand what they are saying to each of us." Where such silences become a recognized and habitual part of the worship they can help the children to lay their minds open to

[1] The kind of music used in the B.B.C. Broadcast Service for Schools will serve as a guide.

the promptings of the Holy Spirit in ways which may be quite impossible by more direct means.

Again, train younger children, quite unostentatiously, to put their hands together and close their eyes, explaining that these simple acts are a way of composing the body and the mind so as to fix our whole attention on Christ alone; and don't be too much concerned to see that the children are doing it properly. If your own hands are together and your own eyes closed, children will follow suit quite naturally; and even if they don't, the sight of your own absorption in prayer will do them a world of good! Let the whole conduct of the service be quiet, unhurried, and full of opportunities for silent prayer and thought under clear guidance from the leader.

Composure

Reverence includes also that leisureliness and composure which allows people time to collect and concentrate their thoughts. Here one or two "Dont's" may be useful. Don't gabble prayers (or allow the children to do so). Don't turn the pages of your book in search of the next prayer while you are still saying the current one! (A few slips of paper at the appropriate places will easily solve that difficulty, which is all part of a careful preparation beforehand.) Don't say "Let us pray for the sick"—and then plunge straight into the prayer on the same breath. Leave the children time to catch up with you and focus their thoughts. These simple rules (which we might call "production points") may sound trite and obvious, but they are broken with sad regularity every day in hundreds of schools and churches.

It is important too, in fostering an atmosphere of reverence, to see that the children are reasonably comfortable. This has a strong bearing on devotion. Don't let them sit or kneel too long on hard floors. Let them vary their position fairly often. In churches children are often compelled to kneel down in pews or at chairs which are too big for them. If you try the effect of kneeling at a sideboard with your nose on the edge or sitting for a long time on a table with your legs dangling, you will readily realize how the large furnishings of a church may need to be adapted to the needs of children's small and active bodies. Standing with bowed head is a perfectly good and traditional attitude for worship and may need to be more often used with children than any other position. If this again seems a trivial matter I can only reply that I have seen the devotional atmosphere of many acts of school worship completely destroyed by inattention to such details.

Interruptions

Above all, avoid intruding on the atmosphere of worship with anything that is bound to strike a discordant note. This is the most commonly broken rule of all. Leave all notices and acts of discipline until the service is over. If the children are gabbling the Lord's Prayer or dragging the hymns, it is best to resist the temptation to stop in the middle of the service and call them to order. Read the lecture afterwards. There is a subtle danger here to which all who have to lead acts of worship and at the same time maintain a certain discipline are subjected. I have often seen a prayer interrupted while a rebellious youth was clouted round the head. It sometimes happens without the prayer even being interrupted! I have seen the announcement of a hymn or a reading turned into the occasion for a cantankerous lecture about bullying, swearing, chalking on the walls, or general slackness in the classroom. I have seen the singing of an unfamiliar hymn suddenly turned into a congregational hymn practice. Such interruptions on a lower plane are the death of worship. Once the service has begun, with silence, let it proceed quietly to a silent finish in complete integrity. This again may sound a trivial point, but the unfortunate results of this kind of practice are far from trivial.

Interest

The other guiding principle in leading worship is all that is embraced under the heading of *Interest*. The Church, in her wisdom, has devised buildings and liturgies which, by their combined assault, both on the senses and on the spirit, engage interest at every point. The drama of the Eucharist, with its changing pattern of reading and prayer throughout the course of the Church's year, is a perfect instance. That should be our model in school worship. It should attract and sustain the children's interest at every stage. There is no virtue in boredom for its own sake! As we have seen, interest will be best maintained by providing every opportunity for the children to take an active part in the service itself. The daily concerns and interests of the children's life should be reflected in their morning worship, so that they recognize the truth that God is deeply involved in everything that they hold important. This will also require the careful planning of our services, so that their pattern and purpose (aided perhaps by a simple link comment here and there) is made clear and interesting to follow. The course of the Church's Year will provide all the "themes" we need, with room for infinite variation; and, if the prevailing thought of the service is explained at the beginning and the progress of the hymns, reading, and prayers closely related to it step by step, the interest will be easily maintained throughout.[1]

Remember, too, the appeal to the eye. Provide some attractive focus on which the children's wandering gaze may come to rest—a cross or a crucifix (preferably the type

[1] This kind of logical and explicit development of an act of worship is well demonstrated in the B.B.C. *People's Service* on the Light Programme.

of crucifix which represents our Lord reigning from the Cross), a seasonal picture, a table with some flowers or candles; anything that has a Godward inflection and will help them to fix their thoughts on God rather than on the honours board, the swimming trophy, or yesterday's arithmetic left over on the blackboard. I once saw this need perfectly illustrated in a small school where at one end of the hall there was a startling display of caricatures by the school humorist, depicting various members of the staff, and at the other a large Medici reproduction of the Sistine Madonna in a beautiful Florentine frame. The assembly of about sixty boys took place in the direction of the caricatures, of which the central one was a telling likeness of the headmaster himself! As he conducted an admirable act of worship I found myself engaged in an absorbing comparison between the caricature and the original, an activity not very conducive to devotion! I imagine many of the boys were similarly preoccupied. There seemed no reason (except that no one had thought of it) why the assembly should not have taken place facing the other way, when the Sistine Madonna would have made a perfect focus of devotion. This again is the kind of apparently trivial detail which can make or mar the whole atmosphere of school worship.

I have said that interest derives largely from active participation. But this does not necessarily mean that children are always to take a leading part. Most children will prefer to have their worship conducted by adults rather than by other children. We can overrate the appeal to children of watching other children perform. Lessons and prayers will generally make a more powerful impression on them if they are well read by someone who can give them their full weight and interpret their meaning and beauty. But occasionally we may let children be responsible for arranging and conducting a whole service—though it should always be under very careful guidance and supervision, so that the school will not be at the mercy of their limited knowledge and choice. But, in my view, it is a mistake to make this a too frequent practice, specially with juniors; because in religion (as in everything else) children are learners, not instructors, and it is good to let them realize that two thousand years of wisdom and authority lie behind the honoured traditions of Christian worship.

Perhaps I may finish by repeating that all this kind of worship, however admirably devised and offered, still remains *private devotion* unless it is related to the worship of the Church, and that we must take every occasion to remind children that in the last resort, we can never offer God complete and acceptable worship unless we are taking our place within the life of the worshipping community of the Church.

NOTE I

THE DIVIDED CURRICULUM

The outstanding weakness of our present educational system is that it has allowed the curriculum to disintegrate into a number of discrete and unrelated "subjects". A man may become a considerable expert in one small field of knowledge and remain (often quite proudly) a complete ignoramus in all the rest. This is what Dean Inge had in mind when he defined the "expert" as "a man who knows more and more about less and less"! In fact this intense specialization has now reached such extraordinary limits that a scholar may devote a whole lifetime of research to the habits of some obscure African beetle and continue in almost total ignorance of other fields of learning. This is bound to destroy any coherent conception of the world as a "Universe". Such a view cannot see the wood for the trees; and this is the reason why so much modern educational theory (in spite of its tremendous strides in technical efficiency) is more concerned with means than ends and can seldom give a satisfactory answer to the fundamental question, "What is the purpose of education?" apart from material equipment for living in a technological age. The Christian view is that the whole field of knowledge—science, philosophy, history, art, and morals—is *one*, and that all knowledge is in the last resort knowledge of God. This is the truth underlying the medieval insistence that Theology is the "Queen of the Sciences". It is only the Christian faith that can give meaning and coherence to education, whether you regard it as pursuit of knowledge or as equipment for effective living; because the ultimate question is bound to be "What is the purpose of the whole business and where is it all leading to?" That question can be answered only "in the light of Eternity".[1]

This is the reason why the Church School (even though its buildings and equipment may not always be of the highest quality) can still give the truest education.[2] It can teach all the so-called "subjects" of the curriculum as a unity, with that necessary Godward inflection which alone can preserve their coherence. I once knew a Biology specialist in a secondary school who, after an agnostic upbringing, became a Christian and was confirmed. He told me that a month or two later he suddenly realized that, in spite of his Christian conviction about God and his purpose in creation, he had continued (simply from force of habit) to teach Biology according to the materialistic and mechanistic view that he had imbibed at the University, and he faced an intellectual crisis. He found that he could no longer

[1] This is more fully treated on pages 10ff.
[2] It is healthy, as well as just, to remember that the older church schools, often stigmatized as dilapidated and obsolete, were pioneers of education in days before the State was prepared to accept responsibility. They deserve a tribute of honour, not reprobation.

go on teaching his subject with what was inevitably an "atheistic" bias. He believed now that Biology was merely a scientific description of God's creative activity and to preserve his own integrity he must be free to express that conviction. This illustrates the dilemma in an acute form.

There must be a close Godward integration over the whole field of knowledge and experience, so that there is no longer a dichotomy (still less a conflict) between what is taught in the Science period and what is taught in the Divinity period and assumed in the School Assembly. This obviously has a close bearing on the whole subject of Worship, and until our educational system is once again (if ever it is) inspired by a theological outlook that gives unity and coherence to the whole field, we must continue to look to the Church school as the one place where education can be, in the Christian sense, complete.

NOTE 2

BOOKS SUITABLE FOR THE SCHOOL ASSEMBLY

PRAYERS

*The Oxford Book of School Worship (S.P.C.K.), 3s. 6d.

*School Worship Day by Day, by R. L. Arundale (S.P.C.K.), 3s. 6d.

Book of Prayers for Schools, edited by Hugh Martin (S.C.M.), 9s. 6d.

The Daily Service (with hymns). Words and Melody (O.U.P.), Words 2s. 3d. and 3s. 3d.; Melody, 4s. and 4s. 9d. Music Edition (Linson Boards) 10s. 6d.

Daily Prayer (Milner White and Briggs), O.U.P., 8s. 6d.

The School Service, D. Starmer Smith (R.E.P.), 6s.

Prayers and Hymns for Junior Schools (O.U.P.), Melody, 4s. 6d.; full music, 8s. 6d.

*Learning to Pray with the Church, H. A. S. Pink (S.P.C.K. and N.S.), 1s.

Common Prayer for Children, Browne-Wilkinson (S.P.C.K. and N.S.), 1s. 9d.

Prayers for School, Church, and Home, T. Grigg Smith (obtainable through S.P.C.K.), 3s. 6d.

A Book of School Worship, N. J. Bull (Harrap), 7s. 6d.

Unto the Hills, R. R. Broackes (for Junior Schools) (S.P.C.K. and N.S.), 7s. 6d.

* Specially suitable for Church Schools.

READINGS

Versions

The Revised Standard Version (Nelson). School Ed., 10s.

The New Testament in English, Ronald Knox (Burns, Oates & Washbourne), 8s. 6d.

The Gospels in Modern English, J. B. Phillips (Fontana Books), 2s. 6d.

The New Testament Letters, J. W. C. Wand (O.U.P.), 7s. 6d.

Letters to Young Churches, J. B. Phillips (Fontana Books), 2s. 6d.

The Young Church in Action (Acts of the Apostles), J. B. Phillips (Geoffrey Bles), 10s. 6d.

Selections

The Little Bible (O.U.P.), 5s. 0d.

Two-minute Bible Readings (S.C.M.), 10s. 6d.

Readings from the Bible for School Prayers, M. Jarvis (S.C.M.), 2s. 6d.

New Testament Lectionary for Schools, T. C. Hermitage (S.C.M.), 1s. 6d.

Two Years' Readings for School Prayers (S.P.C.K. and N.S.), 1s.

The Daily Reading, G. W. Briggs (O.U.P.), 8s. 6d.

The Oxford Book of School Worship contains a good lectionary.

12

Worship and the Adolescent

ALL that we have discussed so far has been fairly straight-forward. Our two main concerns have been, first, our own proper understanding of what prayer and worship are, so that we can reasonably hope to lead our children to a true experience of them; and secondly an insight into the way children's minds work and what their reactions are, so that we can avoid doing undue violence to their growing spiritual life. But in all this we have been able to assume, and rightly, that young children will for the most part be ready to accept our teaching and guidance without a great deal of hesitation or questioning. We shall, even with quite young children, meet occasionally with stubbornness and rebellion, but this will almost always arise from an emotional dislike of some real or imagined restraint, not from a deep-seated rejection. We have considered various ways of handling this kind of superficial hostility, if we can call it that; but given kindness and sympathy children will tend to follow quite readily wherever we choose to lead. One of the things we most need to be aware of is that young children will accept almost without question anything we give them as long as it is emotionally palatable. We should keep this fact in mind whenever we hear the comment (in connection with second-rate hymns or second-rate comics, for example) that children "like that kind of thing". The difficulty is that children are inclined to like and accept almost anything that is confidently presented to them by people they trust and admire. That is why we need to exer-cise such care that, within the limits of their powers of appreciation, we offer them only the best, whether in Christian truth and worship and standards of moral discipline, or in the field of recreation and amusement.

But the onset of adolescence (that is, any time after the age of eleven) confronts us with an entirely new set of problems. We begin now to meet with a healthy resistance, and one that goes deeper than a purely emotional dislike. This is a situation that requires wise and sensitive handling.

An Analogy from History

In his book *Behold the Spirit* (a book about Christian mysticism) the American writer, Alan Watts, draws an interesting picture of the development of the Christian religion down the ages based on the analogy of a child growing up. Though we may not agree with it in detail, this analogy helps to focus the particular problems of adolescence in a most illuminating way and it will be useful to give a summary of it.

During the early centuries of the Church's life, up to the end of the Middle Ages, people were for the most part content to accept without hesitation or question the authority of Mother Church, though generally speaking it did not exert a very marked influence on their manner of life. It was a period of immense faith, yet at the same time a period of barbarism, cruelty, and loose moral standards, in which only individuals here and there (like St Francis of Assisi) stood out as examples of what true commitment to the Christian way does to a man. The picture of late medieval Italy described in, for example, the Memoirs of Benvenuto Cellini, comes as a shock to our twentieth-century mentality. It seems inconceivable that a man like Cellini could combine, without any sense of hypocrisy, a fulsome piety with a quite flagrant immorality, and even ask God's blessing on his lurid escapades of lust and murder. But it need not come as a shock if we recognize that these early ages represent the childhood of the Church, and that it is a characteristic of childhood to accept authority without much question, while remaining largely uninfluenced by it. No one who wants to help young children must be unduly alarmed if they seem to combine (without any sense of incongruity) moments of high spiritual response with times of wilful naughtiness. For them, faith and life have not yet become integrated. That integration is an adult achievement and is in fact the final goal of all religious education. Our understanding of this truth, whether in the childhood of peoples or in the growth of our own children, will save us from a lot of needless misunderstanding and anxiety.

Then there came, during the fourteenth and fifteenth centuries, a great flowering of the human spirit in Europe in the Reformation and the Renaissance. These great movements represent a process of growing up. They are the adolescence of European civilization. The unquestioning acceptance of Mother Church's authority (combined with wilful misbehaviour) gives way now to an attitude far less simple and childish. Note carefully the characteristics of this new period. It was an age of questioning. The new learning and the new science began to throw doubts on the old certainties. There was a wholesale rejection of authority and orthodoxy. Mother Church began to find her children rather troublesome. They wanted to "think for themselves". They "would not be told". It all has a familiar ring for the parents of growing children. But besides the intellectual questioning there was also a great emotional upheaval. Think of the achievements of the first Elizabethan age in England in the realm of the arts. It was an Augustan age of superb poetry and drama; an age of music and the lyric; an age of idealism and intense love of beauty. It was an age of gaiety and keen enjoyment of living—everything that is summed up in the attractive phrase "Merrie England". It was an age of hero-worship, when the great seamen-adventurers (who were little more than pirates) captured the popular imagination as few popular heroes have ever done. It was an age of discovery and exploration, the beginning of that great movement of world conquest which has continued right up to our own generation in the discovery of the Poles and the Ascent of Mount Everest and is now turning its thoughts to the colonization of the Solar System! But at the heart of all this gaiety and adventure, life still remained tentative and questionable, and the careless rapture of living was shot through with acute pessimism and doubt. The Elizabethan "melancholic" (depicted by Shakespeare in such characters as Jacques, and reaching its peak in Hamlet) was a typical figure of the age, hovering between moods of brittle levity and dark despair. The first Elizabethan age in England is an almost perfect picture of the strain and stress of adolescence.

If Alan Watts' assessment is a true one, it suggests that we are now drawing towards the end of that immature period and preparing to embark on a further stage of growing up. We are living in fact at the tail-end of an adolescent age. The next step should be an advance towards adult maturity; and the essence of full adult-hood is the complete co-ordination of Belief and Life. The true adult is the fully integrated personality who has found a faith to live by; not (like the child) a faith accepted unquestioningly but with little overt effect on behaviour; not (like the adolescent) a faith that has to be subjected to constant scrutiny and is continually being re-shaped; but a secure and settled faith that can become a sound basis on which to build the whole structure of life. We can see the slow movement towards this kind of faith in the prevalent impatience with religious humbug or hypocrisy. In the twentieth century (unlike the nineteenth or any previous century) we are not so ready to admit—still less to condone —a dichotomy between what a man professes to believe and what he in fact practises. This underlies the common charge against church people that too often they don't "practise what they preach". You see it in another form when people refuse to be confirmed because they are afraid they cannot "live up to it". The days are long past when a business-man, well known for his dishonesty, could go smugly to church every Sunday with his Bible under his arm in order to set a good example to the lower orders, and yet excite very little adverse comment. Today he would be stigmatized for the humbug he really is and would earn no respect from anybody. This characteristic of "honest-mindedness", though we must not overrate it, is one of the most significant features of the twentieth century's attitude to religion and does point to an important recognition of the need for a faith that informs life. Strangely enough Marxist Communism (itself a very potent "faith") has done much to foster this adult conception by its insistence on the principle that "Theory and Practice are one".

Alan Watts makes the interesting suggestion that the adolescent stage in the development of Christian faith is now slowly passing into the adult stage. In a world of many conflicting faiths (all claiming to be a programme for practical living) there may be fewer adherents for the time being to the Christian way, but they are at any rate, to a greater extent than they were a hundred years ago, people who are seeking a synthesis between Belief and Life. This movement may be seen reflected in the present-day popularity of "mystical" strains in Christianity, of which the Oxford Group Movement (now Moral Re-armament) has been the most outstanding. Mysticism, broadly conceived, may be defined as the immediate apprehension and recognition of God in every moment of experience, and for that reason it as an essentially practical thing and must permeate life to its roots. The Group Movement with its stress on "guidance" and its "absolute" values of behaviour was a rather superficial and facile form of mysticism, but it was closely tied to the practical concerns of daily life in even its most trivial details. The important thing to notice in all recent trends in religion is this growing insistence that faith must be a firm and undisputed foundation for life at large; and when faith and practical living are fully integrated we have reached the stage of adult-hood. This integration, as I have said, is the final aim of all religious education.

Features of Adolescence

As we go on now to consider the problems of adolescence and the goal we are setting ourselves as we try to lead young people to the experience of worship, we shall find this analogy from the history of the Church very illuminating. We will begin by looking at the chief characteristics of the adolescent boy and girl. This is only a very rough and general picture and there is a good deal of minor difference between boys and girls at this age which we shall not try to deal with in details; but in broad outline they follow very much the same pattern of growth.

Questioning

The immediately obvious thing is that adolescence is a time of questioning and stock-taking. The young person is no longer willing to accept passively everything he is told. He wants to test things for himself. Hamlet's famous dictum "This must be scanned" is a perfect expression of adolescent mentality. This may lead, in its turn, to a thoroughgoing rejection of authority, both in the intellectual and the moral sphere, though a good deal will naturally depend on the nature of his earlier experience. Many young people will pass very quietly and quickly through this stage of consolidation; others may go through an acute and prolonged experience of spiritual and intellectual storm and stress. The only convinced "atheist" I have ever met was a boy of thirteen who expressed his views with loud and insolent assurance. But he was quite normal again within two years! He was merely rejecting, for the time being, a God who had been foisted on him too violently by his elders and he showed his growing independence of mind by trying to shock everybody. "Why should I believe this?" "Why should I do that?" "Who says so?"—those are typical adolescent reactions. He becomes impatient with mere unreasoning dogmatism and rebels against regulation and restraint until he is satisfied of its sanctions. The adolescent response to "I'm telling you" is always "Says you!" The reason is obvious. He is beginning to feel his feet as a person and needs to be reassured that he is a person of some importance, quite capable of taking his place side by side with the rest of the world. Actually, at heart, he still feels very insecure and uncertain of himself, and a good deal of this sort of bravado is a kind of whistling to keep his courage up. Sometimes it may lead to rude, self-assertive behaviour that looks like wilful insubordination; it may even take the form of hooliganism. It is altogether a "difficult age" and can easily get out of hand if he meets with harsh or dictatorial treatment.

Adventure

Another feature of this period is the *sense of adventure and exploration*. He likes to experiment and find out things for himself, and he resents any undue interference. In actual fact he needs a good deal of help and guidance, but it must be unobtrusive. Although he resents obvious attempts to influence him, he equally resents complete neglect. The secret of dealing successfully with young people of this age is to keep alongside them sympathetically, ready to offer assistance or comments when they are asked for or obviously desired, but avoiding any kind of dogmatic or superior attitude.

Hero Worship

Then again adolescence is a time of *hero-worship*. The relationship of young children with older people is fairly casual and non-committal. Children like or dislike people, love or detest, only superficially. There is no strong emotional quality about it. With the adolescent this response to people is greatly sharpened and is far more deeply emotional. His admiration or detestation become violent impulses. He will project his growing ideals into some admired person or persons in whom he sees demonstrated the kind of qualities he most wishes to possess himself. It may be a great sportsman or film star; it may be a gangster or some other character, real or fictitious, who typifies his ideal of virility, prowess, domination, or rebellion. With girls this hero-worship is liable to be more intensely personal and charged with deeper emotion. The *grande passion* may involve emotional entanglements which can be very embarrassing for the object of them, and need to be handled with great understanding. One of the most vital concerns of those who deal with adolescents must be to direct into the right channels this urge to worship. We shall deal with it more fully later.

Self-consciousness

A further characteristic of the adolescent is the growth of self-consciousness, in both a good and a bad sense, which is part of his developing sense of self-importance. Self-consciousness in the good sense is the awareness of himself as a person possessing certain powers of mind and body and entitled to take his place in the social framework and to make a valued contribution to the common life, whether of family, school, church, or society at large. But because he is still so unsure of himself and is not certain how he will be accepted in this new rôle, he is also liable to be self-conscious in the less desirable sense, a feeling which is accentuated by certain awkwardnesses in his physical make-up. At this stage in his bodily development he is likely to be gauche and awkward and is often blamed unjustly for clumsiness and lack of physical control for which he cannot really be held responsible. He is "like a bull in a china shop", and his breaking voice and incipient moustache will often add to the impression of gracelessness. He is all too conscious of these awkward elements and will strongly resent any comment on them as an affront to his self-esteem. We must let him find his own way through this embarrassing stage with as little hindrance as possible, forbearing impatient remonstrance and showing no undue awareness of his struggle for equanimity. At all costs avoid needless conflict.

Self-assertion

This growing self-consciousness will often show itself by uncomfortable self-assertion, not only on the physical but also on the intellectual plane. He may become extremely opinionated, pig-headed, impudent, and conceited, and there is very little use in arguing with him. This is a condition that may continue very late into adolescence.[1] We

[1] The late Archbishop Temple once made a revealing comment on this point: "While it is of the utmost importance to pay attention to the general direction in which the minds of the younger generation seem to be moving and the spirit in which they are thinking about the world in which they live, I should like to repeat what I have said before, that no sane person pays the slightest attention to the opinions which they hold. When I was a don at Oxford one of my pupils used, as an habitual expression of strongly held opinion, the phrases 'I shall always believe . . .' and 'I shall never believe . . .'. He continued to use those phrases throughout the four years that I was teaching him, but during that time he inverted the propositions to which they applied." (Pamphlet on *Communism*: William Temple, p. 4.)

should avoid trying to impose ideas upon him and resist the impulse to tell him that he will be more sensible when he gets a bit older! That kind of comment invariably exasperates him or merely drives the rebellion deeper. It is wiser to respect his views, however outrageous, without being the least bit shocked by anything he says, but at the same time to maintain one's own convictions with perfect assurance, saying in effect "Well, that's how *you* see it—this is how *I* see it." It is more than likely that he will be quoting your views as his own within a week! He can be led, but he will not be driven; though even then the leading must be unobtrusive and will derive its force from your own sense of honest conviction rather than from any deliberate effort to influence him.

Gregariousness

As he begins in this faltering way to find his feet in society he discovers an increasing satisfaction in co-operating with other people in various common enterprises. Adolescence is a time of corporate effort and *esprit de corps*. With younger children it is quite different. They are isolated individuals in everything they do. When tiny children play together they are merely individuals amusing themselves in company, so to speak. A typical young children's game is "Follow-my-leader" where, though they are actually playing *together*, there is no real co-operation. They are all doing the same thing at the same time, but they are doing it independently. The team-game, involving the kind of selflessness and discipline which make it possible for a boy to pass the ball and allow another member of his team the glory of scoring the goal, is impossible before children have reached adolescence. I once visited a Christmas party of junior children at which a well-meaning but misguided young woman had devised a programme of competitive games more suitable for a Scout troop or a parish social, and she was deeply hurt and puzzled when she found that the children did not appreciate her efforts and preferred to rush around noisily on their own account! It would have been an admirable programme for twelve-year-olds who are just beginning to enjoy working together in groups and are prepared to make a contribution, even if it is only a small one, to the success of their "side". This illustrates vividly the big advance made at this stage. Adolescence marks the development of "gregariousness", the urge to belong to the group, or the "gang", and to share a common activity with other like-minded enthusiasts. It is all part of his effort to realize his significance in the social set-up. For this reason, as it seems to me, the Scout Movement, with its counterpart in the Guides, is far and away the most imaginative of all the uniformed organizations provided for young people of this age. It harnesses the gang-instinct in the most satisfying way by providing common activities which are focused upon the ideal of being a useful member of society. The Scout is one who is deliberately equipping himself to "be prepared" for any kind of emergency; Scout-craft is a team game at a very high level, and it meets the psychological needs of the adolescent at almost every point.

Altruism

This brings us to the most important characteristic of adolescence—and that is the beginning of Idealism, Altruism, and (in its fullest sense) Love. Side by side with his growing awareness of himself, there comes an awareness of other people, and of their needs and rights. This includes his new attitude towards the other sex. I say "includes" because we sometimes make the mistake of isolating and over-emphasizing the sexual development of adolescence. It is true enough that this looms very large, deriving from the realization of bodily powers which have been lying largely dormant during childhood. (Though we need to remember, in passing, that sex is not always dormant in childhood and quite tiny children may experience strong physical attraction for members of the other sex.)[1] But, where it is given the opportunity of developing healthily, this response to the other sex is only a part—though obviously a very potent part—of his increasing concern for "other people" and should be seen as a growth towards Altruism, or Love in its wider Christian sense of ἀγάπη, that is, sympathetic care and concern for the well-being of others. This will carry with it a respect for the other sex which, wisely guided, will help him to avoid exploiting sex for purely selfish gratification. It is only when sexual attraction is thus combined with altruism that young people will be able to lay the foundations of a happy and stable married life later on.

Standards

All these altruistic trends—the increasing realization of his place in a community of persons, demanding respect for the needs and rights of others, and claiming a contribution from him—confront him with the need for certain standards to live by, social standards as well as personal ones. He is likely to become very critical of wrongs and injustices and begins to formulate, sometimes rather hesitantly, sometimes with extreme assurance, a code of personal and social behaviour. In other words, his "ideals" begin to take shape. He needs then some clear purpose in life to integrate his developing outlook. He is in fact looking for the underlying meaning of the world, and however chaotic and confused his opinions and aims may continue to be for a long time to come, he will not be able to rest content till he has

[1] "As between Oscar Wilde who gave 16 as the age when sex begins, and Rousseau who declared that his blood boiled with it from his birth, my personal experience confirms Rousseau and confutes Wilde." Bernard Shaw, *Sixteen Self-sketches*, p. 113.

reached that "adult" stage (to which we have already referred) of welding all these warring aims and ideals into a comprehensive and coherent philosophy of life. That is what we mean by describing adolescence as a time for the formulation of ideals. The adolescent is by nature a reformer. He can be terribly impatient of the "mess" which other people have made of things and is quite sure that he could make a better job of it himself. This is all to the good and should be given every possible encouragement; but it has its dangers too. The thoughtful adolescent, because of this passionate concern for justice, can become the easy prey of political or ideological programmes which promise to "get things done". He wants to "have a smack" at things on his own account; to "get cracking". These popular phrases express something of his impatience with the world he inherits and his strong urge to put it to rights. Of course, this is something of an ideal picture of adolescence. Not all young people will show strong political or social concern. In many of them this progress towards altruism, which should be a normal development at this stage, will be vitiated by the spurious satisfactions and self-indulgences which our civilization affords, or they may imbibe the prevailing atmosphere of selfish disillusionment which underlies that monstrous post-war confession of indifference, "I couldn't care less". When the onset of idealism is side-tracked into this kind of futile egotism it can produce very unpleasant types—like the Bright Young People of the Twenties and the Teddy Boys and Girls of today. But this only serves to underline the desperate need of all adolescents to discover a "faith" to live by—a set of beliefs that can account satisfactorily for the many problems with which life is beset and offer a practical programme for living, both as individuals and as members of society. In the past many of the more thoughtful and idealistic young people with a strong sense of social concern have tended to find the answer to their quest in Communism or kindred ideologies, rather than in the Church. This should come as a sobering challenge to us who are convinced that only the Christian faith possesses the true and final answer to all they seek; an answer to all the perplexing philosophical problems such as the purpose of man and of the natural order; an answer to all the ethical problems of personal life, and an answer to all problems of social and political action and reform.

This brings us then to the heart of our discussion about Worship and the Adolescent. We have seen repeatedly how worship is the "all-pervading recognition of the absolute worth of God", permeating the whole field of knowledge and experience, intellectual, emotional, and moral. There is no aspect of life, however trivial, that is not embraced in this conception of worship, and in fact it is only such worship that can effect that complete integration, that synthesis of Belief and Life, which we have seen to be the aim of all education. In the last resort all sound education cannot avoid being *religious* education, precisely because it must take account of meaning and purpose in order to provide a cogent basis for the practice of living. It must be concerned with ends as well as means. The only alternative is a blind and aimless drift which can lead to nothing except disaster.

THREE BASIC NEEDS

The immense importance of adolescence is that, where development is allowed to follow a healthy course, the young person is, by the very laws of his unfolding nature, searching for the things we most want him to find in Christian worship. Let us isolate, from the rather diffuse picture we have given of adolescent experience, the three most crucial elements—*Hero-worship*, the *Gang-instinct*, and the *Growth of Altruism*. These in fact summarize very clearly the three basic needs of the adolescent as he tries to find a purpose for his life:

(1) Someone to trust,
(2) Something to belong to,
(3) Something to live for.[1]

It is revealing to study the ways in which the totalitarian movements of our time have succeeded in capturing the allegiance of young people on sound psychological lines by an appeal to those three fundamental needs. Look, for example, at the Nazi movement in Germany. The urge to hero-worship and loyalty to a person was subtly focused on the Führer himself. Hitler was presented, in explicitly Messianic terms, as the hero of all German Youth, the revered Leader and Saviour of his people, and the one focus of all their loyalty, overriding all lesser loyalties to parents, friends, or colleagues. The adolescent urge to belong to a group was given its outlet in the *Hitler Jugend* and the *Hitler Mädel*, based outwardly on the pattern of the Scout movement but fundamentally very different. The purpose of these glorified "gangs" was to guide young people's loyalty to the group into ideological channels, and these movements became recruiting grounds for the young thugs who were later to staff the S.S. and the S.A. and run the extermination camps. Like the Scout movement, they opened up, within the limits of Nazi ideology, opportunities of active service in a cause greater than themselves in which they could feel that they were being "useful members of society." And dominating the whole scene there was the gigantic ideal of National Socialism to which everything else was subordinated—the establishment of the Third

---

[1] I am indebted for this useful analysis to a talk given by the Reverend R. H. Gill, then Secretary of the Church of England Youth Council, at the Youth Conference at Oxford in September, 1950.

Reich, the great empire of the German people, completely united in love and loyalty to their "Saviour", extending the benefits of their *Kultur* to lesser peoples and ruthlessly eliminating all the enemies of sound social order. Here was indeed "something to live for"—and die for if need be. We know only too well how desperately mistaken this whole movement was and how it led the world to disaster; but in spite of all its evils and absurdity it was able to attract the whole-hearted allegiance of millions of young people because it was so skilful in appealing to those three deep-rooted needs of adolescence. It was, however inadequate, a faith to live by.

We may bear this picture in our minds as we go on to consider how the Christian Church possesses, in a far more powerful degree, the means of satisfying these three deep needs.

Someone to trust

In spite of his apparent independence, the adolescent craves for an object of worship, a hero, a man who objectifies his growing conception of what a human life ought to be. In the earlier stages this hero-worship may be concentrated on many different kinds of people—some remote, like a famous sportsman or explorer (some perhaps even fictitious, like Dan Dare), but others in more immediate contact, like the Captain of the First Eleven, the Scoutmaster, or the Curate. It will always be older people whose gifts or achievements he admires and would like to emulate. Of these "heroes" the more immediate ones are obviously the more influential, and anyone who has dealings with young people of this age must be ready to accept, without misunderstanding or abusing it, the tribute of this kind of "worship". They must also recognize that it lays an immense responsibility on them, the responsibility of directing it eventually beyond themselves to the only hero worthy of such veneration. It is an admirable thing when a Curate or a lady worker, a Scoutmaster or a Club leader or a Sunday School teacher, can become a "hero" in this sense. It is impossible to estimate the influence that a priest like the Reverend David Sheppard can exert over his young admirers, simply by the mere fact that a man who has dedicated his whole life to the service of God and the Church can play cricket for England and make a brilliant score in a Test Match! But not every priest can hope to be a David Sheppard, and we need not make the mistake of supposing that athletic prowess is the only way to the adolescent's admiration. Any leader of young people who possesses the qualities of integrity, humour, fair-mindedness, determination, and firm leadership may find himself the object of their adoration. He will then need to look very carefully at the standards he presents to them— not only in his deliberate teaching, but also in apparently trivial things such as his dress, his manner of speech, and his general outlook. Otherwise he may have the gruelling experience of finding his personal slovenliness, favourite expletives, or political prejudices being faithfully reproduced by some youthful admirer!

The same is true of girls as of boys. I remember a young lady-worker in a slum parish in London who believed that it was an important part of her work to set her girls a high standard not only in religious ideals but in matters of personal appearance and self-respect. She dressed tastefully, always wore an attractive hair-style, and was quite masterly in the judicious use of feminine make-up! The result was that she received from the girls the tribute of admiration and imitation more generally given to film-stars; and she was a far more worthy object of their devotion because she typified for them not only standards of personal beauty which they were bound to admire in any case, but also standards of Christian belief and behaviour which were all the more attractive by being exhibited in such a person. Here again, I am not suggesting for a moment that every leader of a girls' club can hope to be a fashion-plate, but if she is to guide young people to the more important objects of admiration she does need to realize that their hero-worship generally begins at these more homely levels.

But in the last resort what young people admire most is character. Their admiration for these more superficial qualities will not survive for long unless, underneath them, they find a character they can trust and respect. What they most need is friendship, and one of the chief difficulties in dealing with younger adolescents is to be able to give them the most intimate possible friendship without allowing it to degenerate into the kind of easy-going familiarity which will forfeit their respect. Many a young schoolmaster or club-leader has had costly experience of this difficulty. There must always be a touch of remoteness in any "hero"—a clear line of demarcation between friendly intimacy and undue familiarity over which young people should not be allowed to step. It is quite impossible to lay down hard and fast rules about this. It can be learnt only by experience. But once it is established a leader will possess great power of engaging the young people's loyalty and confidence without any loss of true intimacy.

It is important, too, that a leader of young people who wishes to earn their respect should know his own mind and have a consistent and firmly-held faith. For this reason a mature adult is generally a better youth-leader than a young person who is still floundering. Adolescents are looking for a "faith", and, though they will be intolerant of dogmatism or any domineering effort to shape them, they are impressed by the kind of person who "knows where he stands" and can give a reason for the hope that is in him. A sixth-form master at a Grammar School, who claimed to be an agnostic, was once discoursing on the familiar theme that children should be taught about all religions and then allowed to choose for themselves when they are old enough, and one of the boys asked him "Which one did you choose, Sir?" That was a perfectly pertinent question without being an impertinent one! The adolescent will respect strongly-held convictions even if he does not accept them; and the testimony of a man who knows what he believes and can give his reasons (even if he is an honest and convinced atheist) will do more to help young people to think creatively than a man who halts waveringly between two (or perhaps many) opinions. For a Christian leader it is important that he should express his own convictions clearly and emphatically whenever the occasion requires; but they will appear not so much in the light of personal views or opinions, but rather as part of his committal to Christ and his Church, an expression of his own adherence to God's truth.

And this brings us to the final objective of all hero-worship, the person of Christ. All our teaching and training of children will be vain and fruitless unless it is pointing them all the time to the supreme Hero who enshrines in his divine person all that is most worthy of admiration and homage in human nature and human achievement. Our Lord possesses, if only we can help young people to see him clearly, every attribute that naturally commands their devotion—virility, courage, physical prowess, profound conviction, humour, idealism, personality, and power. He towers head and shoulders above all other men who were ever considered "great"; and if we can interpret the pages of the Gospels (and especially the story of the Passion) in terms which young people can appreciate they will eventually find there a Hero who sums up and transcends all lesser objects of their admiration.[1] One of the tragedies of Christian educa-

[1] This is admirably achieved in *The Man Born to be King*, by Dorothy Sayers.

tion in the past is that we have so often obscured for young people the true character of Christ, substituting for the real picture a weak, maudlin, and wistful figure, steeped in sentiment and false emotion, which may inspire pity but not admiration. To present our Lord as a pitiable figure, pleading for our attention and wounded by our neglect, is to destroy that feeling of respect, tinged with awe and even bordering on a healthy dread, with which young people are ready to approach him. We need to give a great deal of thought to this whole question of the presentation of the character of Christ.[1] But meanwhile let us be quite sure that if young people are enabled to see him as he really is they will find in him an object of hero-worship and veneration which can shape their whole outlook on the world and colour all their other loyalties.

So no leader of young people will be content to accept as an end in itself the tribute of admiration that they may give to him alone. Many a popular preacher or successful youth-leader has captured the adoring allegiance of his devotees only to find that the whole fabric collapses as soon as his personality is withdrawn. It is only when he is skilful enough to disengage himself and to allow the "worship" to become focused on Christ that he can feel he has succeeded and can confidently pass on his work to a successor who may not be so happily endowed.[2] If we are merely aware of this problem we shall be half-way towards handling it successfully. In the last analysis young people will catch the spirit of devotion to Christ which they see manifested in a beloved leader. If he makes Christ the object of his own worship then the young people will be able to see beyond him and find Christ for themselves.

[1] See also p. 69f.
[2] Cf. the old saying: "A priest is one who draws aside the veil that hides God and loses himself in the folds."

Something to belong to

The second need of the adolescent is a social group to which he can belong, affording opportunities to co-operate with other people in some kind of worth-while activity, preferably altruistic rather than self-regarding. There are plenty of sectional organizations which subserve this purpose—uniformed companies, clubs, guilds, and societies of every kind—but they are necessarily limited in their interests and restricted in their field of activity. There is only one "Society" which in its ideals and activities embraces the whole field of life, personal and social, intellectual, moral, and political—and that is the Church of Christ; and the Church is not so much an organization as an organism, a living embodiment of the whole life and nature of God, in Christ. We have examined the nature of the Church in an earlier chapter and have seen how every baptized Christian is a member of it, inheriting its faith, sharing its worship and warfare, and above all, infused with its "Life".[1] Once we are clear about the true nature of this Divine Society, it becomes obvious that it overrides and comprehends all lesser "groups", and we shall do all in our power to prevent young people from coming to rest in any movement that is only partial and sectional. From the Christian standpoint, a Club or a Scout Troop that regards itself as supplying all that young people need at this stage is offering stones instead of bread.

If membership of the Church is ever to fulfil this all-important rôle of providing for the adolescent a satisfying expression of this desire to "belong", there is obviously need for some very radical changes of emphasis. As things are at present the Church is generally the last place where young people look for this kind of satisfaction. Just as older people often complain that they find more congenial fellowship in

[1] See chapter 2, specially pp. 30ff.

the public house or the bowling club than they do in their local church, so young people may find a more satisfactory outlet for their gregarious needs in social clubs or Scout troops—or, at the lowest level, in the companionship of the streets. Even where uniformed companies or social clubs are closely associated with a Christian congregation, it is the company or the club that generally captures their real interest and allegiance, and the Church is likely to seem an optional "extra"—a flavour added to the soup rather than the basic ingredient! How are we to help the adolescent to find, in the Church's fellowship of worship and action, the ideal "gang" (because that is what it really is), to which he can feel a strong impulse to commit himself?

Part of the answer lies in the kind of approach, from childhood onwards, which we have outlined in the earlier chapters. The more we can help the young child from his infancy to feel that he is a valuable and honoured member of the Family of God, sharing, by virtue of his Baptism, in its privileges and its duties, the more he is likely to recognize without difficulty, when he reaches adolescence, that the fellowship of the Church subsumes and embraces all lesser fellowships included in it. That is why it is so important that he should be brought up within the kind of setting (described in chapter 10) in which all Church organizations find their unity and focus at the altar. A serious weakness in the Church of England is that the subsidiary departments into which the life of a congregation is bound to be divided—the Mothers' Union and the C.E.M.S., the Sunday Schools, companies, and social clubs—are far too often allowed to develop into independent coteries accepted as ends in themselves, so that people are encouraged to think that by belonging to one of these groups they are discharging their duties as members of the Church. This danger is even greater when these lesser units within the Church are allowed to have their own "corporate communion" at different times, so that it would seem to be more important to worship and receive communion as a member of the Mothers' Union or the Youth Club than as a member of the whole Christian congregation. This causes a serious rift in the unity of the Family and fosters the delusion that sectional organizations are more important than the Church itself. The only certain cure for this dangerous situation is some kind of Family Service, preferably a Parish Communion along the lines we have commended, at which all these subsidiary groups should be required to meet together as one; because worship at the altar is the expression of our unity in Christ and cannot admit of divisions in the one Body. Any child who is brought up within the life of such a worshipping community will learn spontaneously, without anyone having to point the moral for him, that the Church comes first and all else is secondary. Under conditions that too often prevail at present it is not surprising that we find difficulty in persuading him of this truth. You cannot teach one thing and practise another—and then expect a child to sort out the truth for himself. This is just another instance of how the most effective teaching is given, not through precept but through practice; not in explicit instruction, but in the thing that is "taken for granted".

Where a child grows up feeling that he "belongs"—and sees everybody else belonging too—it will be much easier for him to give his total allegiance to the Church when he reaches adolescence. He will not feel such a strong urge to break away, because his roots will already have gone deep. Where a young person comes into the life of the Church at a later age and there are no such roots to secure him, he will still be profoundly influenced by the same two factors —the friendly welcome into the communal life of the Family which makes him feel that he "belongs", and the subordination of the lesser "groups" he may join to the larger loyalty of Parish, Diocese, and the Church at large. While he is still a child he will accept most of this without question. His simple social needs will be provided for in various week-day activities and he will regard these as a happy and normal part of the social life of a Church whose chief business is worship. But as he advances into adolescence we must help him to discover, within the full life of the Church, a satisfying outlet for his growing social impulses and his desire to co-operate with other people in useful activity. How is this to be done?

It is a sad thing that for so many young people their Confirmation is merely the prelude to an anti-climax. During the time of preparation they have been given something to look forward to; sometimes perhaps their hopes have been mistakenly raised and they have been led to expect some exciting emotional experience which will shake their life to its foundations. We must do all we can to guard against this peril. In such a case they are desperately disappointed that their Confirmation leaves them feeling much the same as they did before; and, when they are no longer sustained by the interest and excitement of anticipation and the experience itself has proved a disappointment, they are very prone to fall away. The danger is increased by the fact that they may be—and generally are—left completely high and dry after their Confirmation. They are rather like jellyfish carried in on the tide and left stranded on the beach, helpless and inactive, with nothing to *do*. Somehow we have got to get them back into the sea again, so that they can live a fully active and useful life in their proper element. In other words it is the business of the Church to provide these young people with some kind of useful employment, some job of work, some actual share in the life of the Church in which their urge to "serve" can find a satisfactory outlet.

I am not overlooking the fact that a great deal of the

practice of religion—prayers, communion, the sacrament of penance, and the disciplines of daily life—is a personal matter, and many of these young people will find a strong personal religion that will hold them fast to the Church even if they find no outlet there for social and altruistic impulses. But personal religion of this kind is obviously in danger of becoming a self-centred individualism. Christianity is by its very nature a social as well as a personal religion. We should do all in our power to encourage Church people, young and old alike, to find a sphere of Christian service wider than what is generally comprehended under the term "church work". They must stand for their Christian convictions and witness to their faith in all the various claims of industrial and commercial life, in their political affiliations and social concerns, as well as in their homes and friendships. Young people should certainly be helped to realize that Christian service to the community may often best be given by taking a strong and active part in the life of their Trade Union, by bringing Christian convictions to bear on their political concerns, by exercising their vote from Christian motives of justice and love and not from motives of self-interest. At the simplest level of all, such service can be given through honest and painstaking work, offered to God as part of our worship. In fact it seems likely that, amid collapsing standards of integrity and conscientiousness and even common honesty in the field of industry, the outstanding mark of the young Christian worker will in future be a recognizable quality of conscientiousness in simply doing his job well. It is at this point that the non-Christian should be able to see clearly demonstrated the difference that Christian conviction makes. For a Christian every part of his life—home, job, recreations, and political interests—should be permeated with an obvious and unmistakable social concern.

But when all that is said, it still remains true that young

people on the threshold of adolescence will require a more immediately tangible and concrete expression of this social interest; and they are likely to understand the wider implications of it later on if they are given opportunities of exercising it at first within the setting of the Church's immediate life. That is what I mean by suggesting that all young persons who have been confirmed should be given—or helped to find—a definite job of service under the aegis of the Church. At the moment we seem to have very little to offer them. A boy may sing in the choir or serve at the altar, or take some part in the work of the Sunday School; for girls, Sunday School teaching is often the most we have to suggest and only a small number will feel called upon to respond. It is a very limited field and cannot accommodate more than the merest handful. The rest are left with nothing specific to do, and it is hardly surprising that they either look for opportunities of service outside the Church or remain blankly indifferent and eventually lapse.

I suggest that we should go to great trouble to provide all young persons at their Confirmation with a specific piece of active service within the Church's life, and to lay it upon them as a necessary part of their Christian vocation. Some will already be choristers or servers or Sunday School teachers. Some may find jobs as sidesmen, bell-ringers, decorators, or keepers of the churchyard. Others may be encouraged to assist in various capacities at week-day organizations and uniformed companies for younger children, collecting subscriptions, organizing canteen, or helping with the programme of games. A Sunday School Fellowship of the kind I have described on page 131 will provide numerous interesting jobs for young people in which they can feel that they are directly serving the Church and society at large. A youth club, with the right kind of encouragement, can organize all kinds of valuable assistance. All its activities—dances, dramatic productions, jumble

14

sales—can be helped to subserve the chief purpose of the Church's life, that is to bring others into the worshipping fellowship; and any kind of money-raising effort (clearly recognized as a necessary economic condition of carrying on the Church's main work) should enlist their interest and support. Young people will respond very readily to this kind of challenge if they are helped to see the fundamental value of it. In addition there are all the different kinds of service within the life of the Christian family which we considered in chapters 8 and 9, many of which could prove a suitable undertaking for young adolescents.

But beyond this restricted sphere of parochial activity there are wider spheres of Christian social concern which we can bring to their notice. Because God is the supreme Ruler of the whole universe and Christ is the Lord of all life, all civic and social programmes are for a Christian part of the life of worship. The Lambeth Conference of 1948 issued six Injunctions, addressed to Church people, summarizing the principal ways in which they should "give distinctive witness" to their faith. The fifth of these Injunctions lays it upon Church members to give "personal service to Church and community". The note of "personal" service is most significant. The Welfare State is now doing, rather impersonally, so much of the work of "love" (or "charity" in the true sense) that was originally done by the labour of voluntary Christian associations. It is strange that in a State which does really believe (as Socialism has always done) that the welfare of people is paramount, nevertheless the system produced by the application of Socialist principles is so inclined to be impersonal and remote. There is obvious need for the Welfare State to be supplemented by Christian insights concerning the eternal value of human personality and the final purpose of Man. This will have a marked influence on the Christian's approach to secular society and social needs. It means keeping a steady vision of all people as "persons" equally valuable in God's eyes, and that will profoundly affect the spirit in which Christians will view and handle all questions of social service. Many of the most crying needs of the past are now being supplied by official state-aided services, and we must be immensely thankful for these basically Christian provisions, even when they are administered by a rather cold and aloof officialdom. But there are still many areas of human need which are not being met by any official machinery, and this opens up wide opportunities for voluntary Christian service to society. In the well-known Report on "Voluntary Action" sponsored by Lord Beveridge in 1948 there are a number of proposals for organizing voluntary services, possibly operating through the Citizens' Advice Bureaux, to undertake acts of love and assistance which are not yet included in the official machinery of State aid and are not covered by any insurance schemes; the kind of services that cannot be obtained by paying for them. In every parish there are numbers of old and lonely people (not necessarily connected with any church) to whom a weekly visit, specially from a friendly young person, would be a veritable godsend. Often they are in need of very simple kinds of help, which a group of young Church people could well organize under the guidance of their Vicar. It may be a little cleaning or dusting; it may be reading to them for an hour or just dropping in for a friendly chat; it may be writing a letter or helping them to fill up some of the innumerable forms that harass them so much; it may be cooking an occasional meal or doing some shopping; it may be no more than just creating a memorable interlude of companionship in their lonely existence. This kind of service, undertaken regularly and regarded as a definite commitment, might become a carefully organized feature of parish life, in which young and old alike could be expected to take a share. If the vicar is in close touch with the local organization of social services they will be able to provide him with jobs of this kind almost without limit. There is no need for them to be undertaken solely for the purpose of evangelism; that might in fact detract considerably from their value, because the recipients of such kindnesses could easily resent what they might consider an ulterior motive. The mere fact that the Church cares enough for people, irrespective of their religious profession, to want to help them in this way will do more to commend the Christian religion than any amount of pious talk. Other kinds of service mentioned in the Beveridge Report include such things as Blood Transfusion, Children's Holiday Camps, sitting in for young married couples with babies, so as to allow them an evening out together (or perhaps to allow them to get to Evensong together), besides the usual claims of social clubs and guilds, not necessarily under the aegis of the Church. The field is immense and we do not need to look far beyond our own noses to find an opportunity for service of this kind that could be undertaken in any parish by a group of well-disposed young people.

In fact, if we really give our minds to this problem, there is no reason why any young Christian who really means business should not find in the community of the Church a thoroughly satisfying fulfilment of his urge to "belong" and to serve; and the share he may take at the same time in other subsidiary social groups will be all the more valuable because he can accept them as part of his total service of God—of "worship" at its fullest. By finding such an experience of fellowship and service in the first instance within the community of the Church he will be better equipped, when he is older and more responsible, to carry over this spirit of Christian social concern into his political and industrial activities. The direction of all religious educaton is from the particular to the general, and this is a case in point.

Something to live for

We have considered over and over again in the course of this survey how only the Christian religion can supply a complete and satisfactory answer to all the perplexing problems of life (personal and social) and give effective expression to all altruistic motives. It is the one and only "world view" that can integrate the war-ring factors of human personality (seen so clearly in the turmoil of adolescence) and give meaning and purpose to human life. Just as the objective of National Socialism, which commanded the allegiance of so many young Germans as something to live and die for, was the establish-ment of the Third Reich, the domination of the German people over the whole world, so the objective of the Christian Church is the Kingdom of God, the establish-ment of God's Rule over the whole world. "Thy Kingdom come, on earth, as it is in Heaven". It is impossible to conceive any objective greater than that. All the lesser pur-poses to which people may devote their lives have no lasting value unless they are part and parcel of the one all-pervading purpose that underlies creation. This is God's world—it is his plan that is being worked out in it. It will not work according to any other laws except the laws of God, as we are constantly realizing to our cost in the disorder of human lives and the chaos of the world. God's purpose is that all human souls should find their happiness in fellowship with himself and there is no happiness apart from him. It is only when God is recognized as King that the various parts of the jigsaw will fall into place and make a coherent picture. "Seek ye first the kingdom of God and his righteousness and all these things shall be added unto you" (Matt. 6.33).

That is the huge setting within which we must help young people to view all the conflicting claims and impulses of their life—the setting of eternity, which alone can put things in their proper perspective. It is a totalitarian claim upon them, far more exacting than the claims of any political ideology, and carrying with it the same challenge of complete dedication and self-sacrifice. The Church, if it is to win the respect and loyalty of young people, must offer an uncompromising challenge of "blood, toil, tears, and sweat". The best of them will not be attracted by an easygoing programme of personal salvation, bright services, and pleasant social intercourse, which is what they too often regard the Church as there to provide. But offer them a struggle against the entrenched forces of evil, both in themselves and the world, in which God is enlisting the help of human agencies and fortifying them with his own power; let them see that God is the Lord of all life, concerned not only with what goes on in Church and Sunday School, but with all the baffling problems that make up the social and international scene—housing, employment, industry, education, the fight against disease, local government, political enterprise, international relations, war, and the future of the atomic age—let them come face to face with all this, and they will find a *cause* to which they can dedicate all their powers of mind and body in the service of God and the world at large. This, as we have so often reminded ourselves in the course of this study, is the Worship of God at its highest, and there is nothing beyond it. Here indeed is the one and only "something to live for" which will stretch them to the furthest limit and keep them fully employed to the end of their life and beyond.

13

The Necessity of Right Belief

WE have ranged widely over the whole field of Worship and it will be helpful to put the completed picture into focus. We began by examining the roots of Worship in Christian theology and in the Christian Cultus. We acknowledged the absolute necessity of the Church as the spring of all Christian devotion, which has its only true centre in the sacrament of Holy Communion. We studied the principles governing both corporate worship and personal prayer, and then went on to consider some of the practical problems of introducing children to the practice of devotion. Perhaps some of us found these considerations a challenge to our own spiritual life. We saw the enormous importance of meeting children's questions (even the most trivial ones) with assurance and sensitivity, avoiding negative and disturbing metaphors, and forestalling where we can the fears and misconceptions which can so easily upset for life the whole balance of their religion. We considered ways in which, from his earliest babyhood, the child can be intimately related to the worshipping community of the Church and helped to accept his place quite naturally within it; and we stressed the responsibility of the whole congregation to ensure that this is done. We also explored the contribution that the Day School, especially in the morning assembly, can make to the child's growth in common worship and private prayer, with the warning that in all except church schools this should be regarded as a *preparatio evangelii* and not as any kind of substitute for worship in the Christian community. We ended our survey in the last chapter by considering how the Christian religion, truly presented, can meet the most deep-seated needs of the adolescent boy and girl as they seek a firm faith for the whole of life from beginning to end.

Although that last chapter was devoted to the characteristic problems of adolescence, it is also a picture of how, within the life of the Catholic Church, God satisfies the spiritual hunger of all human souls at every stage of adult life. Adolescence is only that stage in the process of growing up when the desires and aspirations which characterize the mature man or woman first begin to take shape. During adolescence the isolation and self-sufficiency of childhood, under healthy and favourable conditions, give place to a sense of community and its accompanying altruism. After that, as the young person slowly advances into more mature adult life, there is no further development in his fundamental physical and spiritual endowments. There is no further unfolding of innate powers. Adolescence is (as the word itself implies) the process of becoming "adult", and for the rest of his life he will be, ideally speaking, engaged in the task of stabilizing and consolidating the general attitude to life which he acquires then. That is why it is so important that he should find the right direction at the onset of maturity. That is the reason, too, why there is no need to add a further chapter on "Worship and the Grown Man". The same truths apply at every future stage. From adolescence to manhood and right down to old age there can be no further change in his fundamental nature as a human being, compared with the revolutionary change from childhood to adolescence. Whatever development takes place later will be development in depth rather than in kind.

We have seen how the essential mark of mature "adulthood" is a clearly formulated synthesis between Belief and Life. The tragedy is that so many grown-up people fail to achieve this synthesis, chiefly because they never find a faith at all. There are physically mature men and women who have never passed successfully through the stage of adolescence and who remain all their lives at a childish level of mentality—self-centred and self-absorbed, seeking only their own ends in virtual isolation, quarrelsome, sulky, given to "tantrums" or the sulks whenever they are frustrated, emotionally unstable and erratic. Perhaps more people than we realize, sometimes highly educated and cultured people, never succeed in emerging from the chrysalis of childhood. This may explain why so many international disputes are conducted in a spirit which savours more of the nursery than of the study! We must bear this in mind, because—though it should be the natural and normal experience of every adolescent to find a new centre of gravity outside himself (and an important part of the Church's business to assist him in finding it)—we should make a serious mistake in imagining that all of them do. It is true that for such people, the experience of "growing up" may, even quite late in life, come through religious conversion; but it can only come when by some such means they have made what Mrs Herman has called the "journey from self to God".[1]

Again, many people who do acquire in adolescence a certain measure of altruism and idealism may still fail to find a satisfying purpose to live for and the power to carry it out. They are liable to become disillusioned and cynical, or else to throw all their energy into humanistic movements such as the Ethical Societies or the Communist party. Moreover, there is always the danger that their social concern (for want of a world-embracing outlook) may become restricted to some narrow and particular "fad", such as Drink or Vivisection or Blood Sports, and that they may remain largely insensitive to the rest of the field of human tragedy and divine purpose. It is only when a man sees the

[1] E. Herman, *Creative Prayer* (James Clark).

world steadily as God's world, with an underlying purpose for Man that will find its fulfilment only in eternity, that he will be able to get a sane and balanced view of the whole human scene. This is what St Thomas Aquinas described as seeing the world *sub specie aeternitatis*—and that (as we have seen) is the essential note of all worship.

Without such a comprehensive "world-view" no man can achieve a complete "adult" synthesis of belief and practical living, because he is bound to leave large areas of life unaccounted for in his philosophy and have no answer to the practical demands they make on him. He will be hampered by "blind spots", and to that extent he will fail to become fully adult. Only the Christian Religion and the Worship of God can bring him "unto a perfect man". This confronts us once again with that most important factor in Christian Worship—one which we have noted several times in passing, but which I should like to make the final emphasis of this book—and that is the absolute necessity of Right Belief. True Faith is the only secure foundation of true Worship in the sense in which we have defined it.

This is a hard saying in an age like our own when so many high-minded people feel that the Christian Faith has been discredited and made obsolete by man's growing mastery of the material world. "Glory to Man in the highest, for Man is the master of things", wrote Swinburne in the heyday of Victorian "Progress"; and in spite of the abyss of doubt and disillusion that has opened at our feet during the last half century (when we have had so much cause to question whether man can ever safely be master of *things* till he is master of *himself*) we still cling frantically to the hope that, given better education and improved techniques, man is perfectible without recourse to God at all. The great mass of secular educational theory is vitiated by this false hope, which is a complete contradiction of the Christian belief about man.[1] It is revealing to study the expressed aims of modern education in so far as they have become divorced from Christian conviction. It is a confused scene. There is no one consistent view and they are all limited to purely human and this-worldly values. The *Vocational* (or *Economic*) *View* of Education, for example, regards it as primarily providing technical equipment for doing a useful job of work in the world—a most essential part of any system of education, as no one would dare deny. But it raises the question, Is work the only purpose of a man's existence? The *Cultural View* lays its main stress on the "problem of leisure" and regards the chief purpose of education as providing satisfying cultural outlets for that more important part of a man's existence (and one that will loom even larger with the advance of automation)—the spare time when he is "free to live". But again we may ask, Is man here only to enjoy himself, however high the level of his cultural interests may be? The *Political View* isolates the idea of Education for Citizenship—and we have seen something of the dangers of this very partial view in the educational systems of Nazi Germany and international Communism. The *Humanist View*, based on the conviction that man is essentially "good" and only needs the right kind of nurture in order to achieve perfect control of himself and the world, sees in education a complete panacea for all the ills and frustrations that beset human life. Other "aims" of this kind are constantly being enunciated (I once saw a pamphlet entitled "Education for Sanity", which one might have hoped could be taken for granted!); but there is no one coherent objective at present informing the whole educational field. It is a chaos of conflicting aims, each of which

[1] Cf. C. E. M. Joad, *The Recovery of Belief* (Faber). Dr. Joad, a life-long humanist, was converted to Christianity because he found in the Church the only institution that was realistic about "sin" and had power to deal with it effectively.

(like the Divided Curriculum)[1] isolates one aspect of education to the virtual exclusion of the others. They are all partially true, but need some overall objective which can weld them together into a single sustained purpose. It is my own firm assurance that only the Christian view of Man can put all these broken fragments together and see the problem as a whole. You cannot isolate one aspect of man's nature and ignore the rest. There is no such thing as Political Man or Economic Man. There is only Man. All these ideas see man purely as a creature of this finite world and stop short at the most important point of all—the moment of his death. They take no account at all of man's purpose and destiny on the other side of death. Their objective is limited purely to the exigencies of the material world. But, in the realm of purpose, death is surely the most crucial factor of all, because it is not until you have come to terms with death and have at least some conception of the purposes that may lie beyond it, that you can begin to make any sense of what things in this world are likely to mean. Only Christian education, with its gaze firmly fixed on eternity, can hope to put the shattered fragments together and, while giving full weight to all these other partial aims of education, equip a man for that great encounter with God which is the sole purpose of his creation. If we wanted to express in a phrase the objective of Christian education we might call it Education for the Kingdom of God, or, if you like, Education for Eternity. We might even call it Education for Worship.

So Christian belief about God and Man and the underlying purpose of the created order goes right down to the roots of all educational concern, theoretical and practical. There is all the difference in the world between any view that tries to find the meaning of man's being in the few

[1] See page 170.

years between the cradle and the grave and one which computes the value of everything in life by looking at it within the vast perspective of eternity. This brings into sharp focus the inescapable necessity of Right Belief. No man can live wisely or profitably for five minutes of his inestimably precious life unless he recognizes clearly the purpose for which he has been put here and the goal of all his striving. Otherwise he is like a man pushing a rowing boat out into the Atlantic Ocean, without oars, compass, map, or provisions, and hoping to make a successful voyage to nowhere in particular! Right Belief is as vital and practical as all that.

No one has ever expressed more clearly this absolute claim of Right Belief than the late Archbishop William Temple. It is an emphasis that runs throughout all his teaching. Perhaps I can best underline this truth by summarizing very briefly the substance of an address he gave to the York Diocesan Conference in 1936, when he defended the necessity of the creeds against those who would maintain that goodwill is more important than specific belief. It is probably true, the Archbishop admitted, that the Church has tended to lay what may appear excessive stress on doctrine compared with the stress it has laid on practical conformity to the teaching of Christ; and yet it is most necessary that the Church should safeguard her belief by taking this stand on a carefully formulated doctrinal basis which her children should be required to accept. "Theological and historical propositions", he said, "should be the basis of church membership, rather than some simple expression of moral aspiration. It is often said that what a man believes is unimportant; that what matters is his life. But his belief is at least part of his life, and if the word 'belief' is taken seriously it is the most important part." If Belief in God means putting trust in God (and such trust is an integral part of worship) then no sane person can say that belief does not matter. No doubt there are many people who are quite ready to express their belief in the language of the creeds who are nevertheless further from the intention of the creeds than others who refuse to express their belief in that way. "None the less, a man's refusal or consent puts him on one side or the other of a watershed. The Rhine and the Rhone rise close together, but one flows to the North Sea and the other to the Mediterranean. So a man who refuses to confess, for example, the Deity of Christ may in fact be nearer to perfect fellowship than another who consents to confess it. Yet the former stands on the side of the watershed whence the waters flow down to lose themselves in the arid desert of Pantheism and pure Immanentism, whereas the other stands on the side of the watershed whence flows the stream of Catholic tradition."

These wise words deserve careful pondering. The Christian Religion is (to use a phrase of Sir Edwyn Hoskins) "lashed to historical moorings". It stands or falls, not by the quality of its moral precepts, but by the truth or falsity of certain historical events from which the value of its teaching derives. Did Christ really live? Was he really God made man? Did he really rise from the dead? Did he really give us the Church and promise that his Spirit would dwell in it and guide it into all truth? It is in the answer to such questions that the value of his teaching finally resides. Christianity is concerned with what God has done and is still doing in history—the great Acts of God—rather than with inspired guesses, moral exhortations, or pious hopes. It claims to be in the realm of fact, not of speculation; and the first step in all true worship must be to acknowledge the facts. This will not necessarily involve unassailable intellectual certainty about them. While we still "walk by faith and not by sight", there must always be an element of blind trust about any act of faith.[1] It is what someone has described as committing yourself to the highest hypothesis, or what Studdert Kennedy, in homelier terms, called "betting your life on God." But our Lord promised that those who did thus commit themselves would come at last to assurance. "If any man willeth to *do his will*, he shall *know* of the teaching whether it be of God or whether I speak from myself" (St John, 7.17, R.V.). Treat the Christian faith *as though* it were true, whatever hesitations you may have about it; do faithfully what it requires of you—and your doubts will eventually merge into the certainty that here, in complete dedication to God through Christ, is the answer to man's agelong quest. It is only within the context of such belief that we can hope to offer God that pure and perfect Worship which is the sole purpose of our creation.

There is one further aspect of this need for Right Belief which has an intimate bearing on the whole thesis of this book about training children in worship. Unless our worship is securely founded on Christian belief then, however advanced our own spiritual attainments may be without such faith, we can never be certain of inducing in our children that same temper of devotion. The very attitude of worship—with all its practical accompaniments—derives its only sanctions from the Faith; and, although individual persons here and there may exhibit a profound devotion without accepting the truths that alone justify it, they will have nothing that can be readily communicated to their children. Spirituality, unless it is enshrined in some tangible

[1] This does not involve the capitulation of reason. The element of intellectual assent lies in the reasonable acceptance of authority. We trustfully swallow the doctor's pills, not because we know how they work, but because we have good reason to accept his authority. Much the same is true of our acceptance of the authority of the Church of Christ.

"form", is not communicable and is easily dissipated. The tradition of Faith in which it is embodied is the only sure channel of communication. And so I finish this book about training young people in worship with one last quotation from Archbishop Temple's address in defence of the creeds, the final sentence of his brilliant analysis of Belief: "A body of Christians who are most sanctified, yet who refuse or are unable to accept the Catholic Faith, will be unable to transmit to subsequent generations the power to which their own sanctity is due."

BV 4561.2 .W54 1957
Williams, John Gordon.
Worship and the modern
child